Best Editorial Cartoons of the Year

DRAPER HILL
Courtesy Detroit News

BEST EDITORIAL CARTOONS OF THE YEAR

1997 EDITION

Edited by
CHARLES BROOKS

PELICAN PUBLISHING COMPANY
Gretna 1997

Library of Congress Serial Catalog Data

Best editorial cartoons. 1972-
   Gretna [La.] Pelican Pub. Co.
   v. 29 cm annual-
"A pictorial history of the year."

   1. United States—Politics and government—
1969—Caricatures and Cartoons—Periodicals.
E839.5.B45   320.9'7309240207   73-643645
ISSN 0091-2220   MARC-S

Manufactured in the United States of America
Published by Pelican Publishing Company, Inc.
1101 Monroe Street, Gretna, Louisiana 70053

Contents

Award-Winning Cartoons   7

The Clinton Campaign 15

The Dole Campaign 41

Ross Perot 51

Politics 57

Congress 73

Foreign Affairs 81

The Economy 101

Health 113

The Family 123

Welfare and the Poor 131

The Military 137

Education 143

Crime 151

Canada 163

Air Travel 169

Sports 175

. . . and Other Issues 185

Past Award Winners 203

Index of Cartoonists 205

Award-Winning Cartoons

1996 PULITZER PRIZE

JIM MORIN

Editorial Cartoonist
Miami Herald

Born January 30, 1953, in Washington, D.C.; graduated from Syracuse University, 1976; cartoonist for the Beaumont *Enterprise* and *Journal,* 1976-77, the Richmond *Times-Dispatch,* 1977-78, and the Miami *Herald,* 1978 to the present; syndicated internationally by King Features; winner of the Oveseas Press Club Award, 1979 and 1990, the H.L. Mencken Award, 1990, the National Cartoonist Society Award, 1992, and the Berryman Award of the National Press Foundation, 1996; author of three books.

1995 NATIONAL SOCIETY
OF PROFESSIONAL JOURNALISTS AWARD
(Selected in 1996)

MICHAEL RAMIREZ

Editorial Cartoonist
Memphis Commercial Appeal

Born in Tokyo, Japan; graduate of the University of California at Irvine; former editorial cartoonist for the Newport *Ensign* and the San Clemente *Daily Sun* and *Post;* cartoonist for the Memphis *Commercial Appeal,* 1990 to the present; syndicated to 950 newspapers by Copley News Service; winner of the Pulitzer Prize, 1994, and the H.L. Mencken Award, 1995.

BRIAN GABLE

Editorial Cartoonist
Toronto Globe and Mail

Born in Saskatoon, Canada, 1949; studied fine arts at the University of
Saskatchewan; graduated from the University of Toronto, 1971; former
art teacher; former editorial cartoonist for the Brockville *Recorder* and
Times and the Regina *Leader-Post;* presently editorial cartoonist for the
Toronto *Globe* and *Mail;* previous winner of the National Newspaper
Award of Canada, 1986.

1996 NATIONAL HEADLINERS CLUB AWARD

JIMMY MARGULIES

Editorial Cartoonist
The Record, New Jersey

Graduate of Carnegie Mellon University in fine arts, 1973; editorial cartoonist for Journal Newspapers, 1980-84, the Houston *Post,* 1984-90, and the *Record, New Jersey,* 1990 to the present; syndicated by King Features / North America Syndicate; winner of the Fischetti Award (opposite page), 1996.

1996 FISCHETTI AWARD

JIMMY MARGULIES

Editorial Cartoonist
The Record, New Jersey

1996 OVERSEAS PRESS CLUB AWARD

JACK OHMAN

Editorial Cartoonist
The Oregonian

Born September 1, 1960, in St. Paul, Minnesota; attended the University of Minnesota; while in college his cartoons were syndicated by the Chicago Tribune— New York News Syndicate; editorial cartoonist, the *Oregonian,* 1983 to the present; cartoons appear in 175 newspapers; comic strip, "Mixed Media," syndicated by Tribune Media Services; author of six books; raised $30,000 for the families of the Challenger astronauts through sales of his cartoon on the tragedy.

Best Editorial Cartoons of the Year

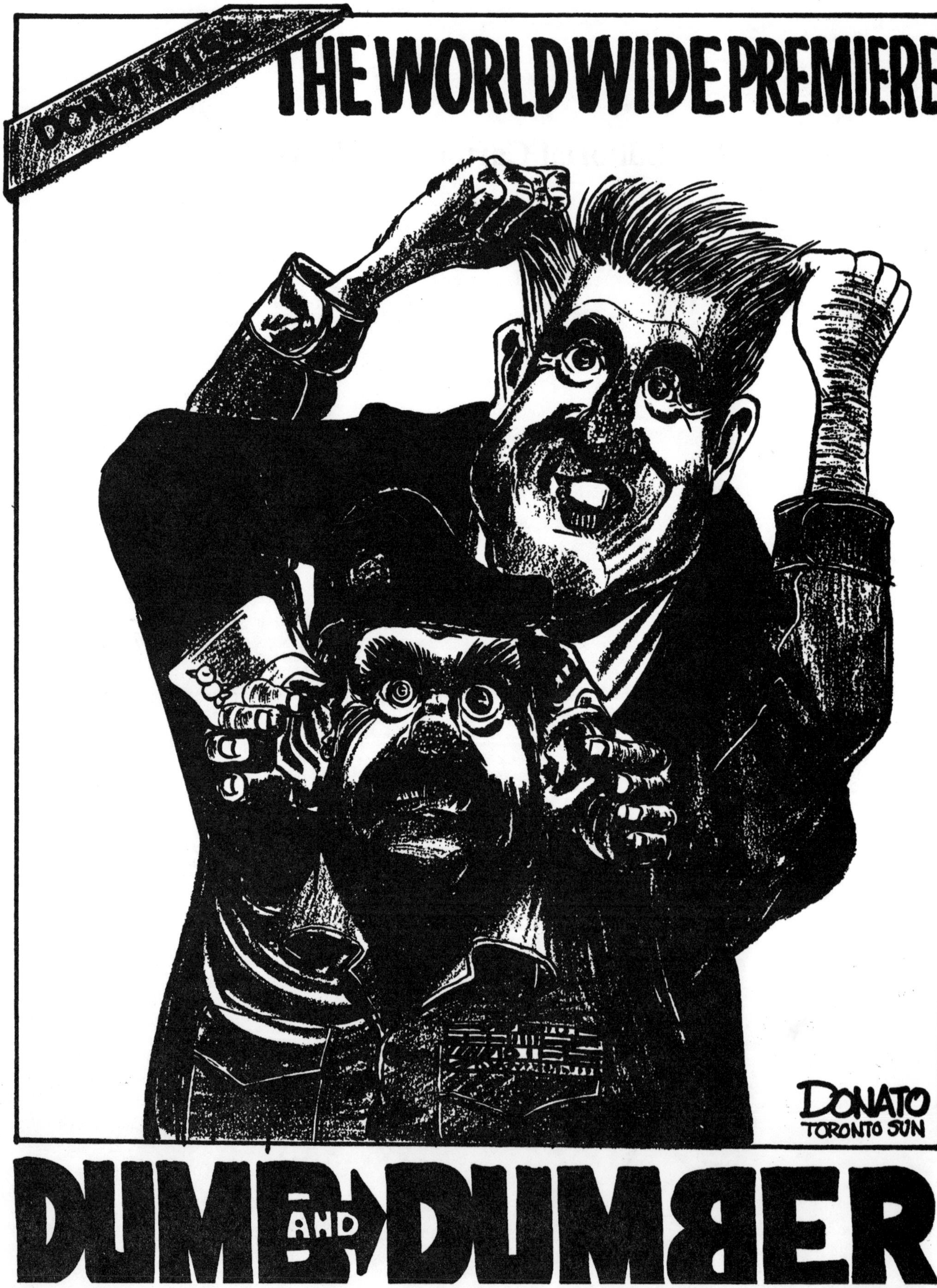
DON'T MISS
THE WORLD WIDE PREMIERE
DONATO
TORONTO SUN
DUMB AND DUMBER

ANDY DONATO
Courtesy Toronto Sun

The Clinton Campaign

Sounding like a conservative Republican, President Clinton kicked off his re-election campaign in an effective State of the Union speech. He endorsed moral values and announced that "the era of big government is over." As the year unfolded, the Republicans accused Clinton of stealing their ideas, but from the start his lead in the polls was solid.

Questions about Whitewater, Travelgate, Filegate, the Dick Morris sex scandal, and the veto of a bill to ban partial abortions did not seem to bother voters, nor did charges of illegal campaign fund-raising by the Democrats.

After several of his friends were sent to jail, the President was asked if he would promise not to pardon them in the future, but he declined to commit himself. The Democrats returned nearly two million dollars in campaign contributions from questionable sources, much of it foreign.

In November Clinton was returned to office in a clear-cut victory. He won 31 states and 379 electoral votes to Republican Bob Dole's 19 states and 150 electoral votes. Clinton's move to the political center after the 1994 congressional elections had paid off.

DICK LOCHER
Courtesy Chicago Tribune

GARY MCCOY
Courtesy Suburban Journals

BRIAN DUFFY
Courtesy Des Moines Register

CLYDE WELLS
Courtesy Augusta Chronicle

GLENN MCCOY
Courtesy Belleville News-Democrat (Ill.)

JOHN TREVER
Courtesy Albuquerque Journal

DICK LOCHER
Courtesy Chicago Tribune

STEVE MCBRIDE
Courtesy Independence Daily Reporter (Kans.)

Let me make it clear... this office can not be bought!

KIRK WALTERS
Courtesy Toledo Blade

MADE IN TAIWAN

MADE IN CHINA

MADE IN INDONESIA

MARK BREWER
Courtesy The Hour (Conn.)

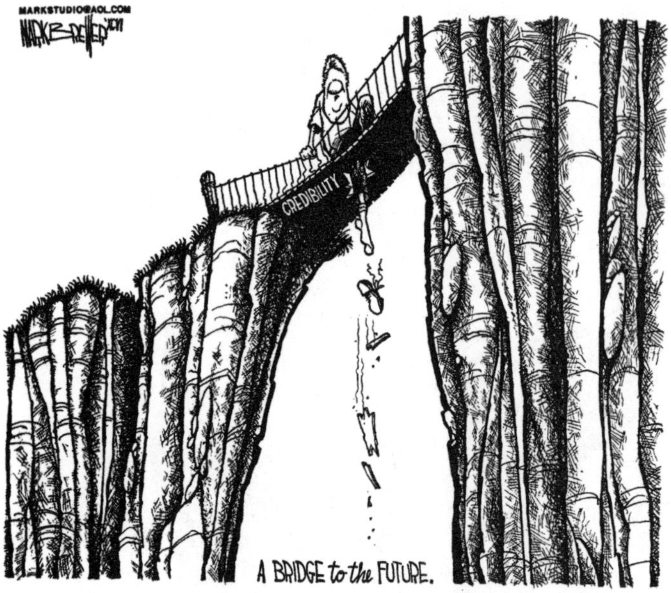
MARKSTUDIO@AOL.COM
CREDIBILITY
A BRIDGE to the FUTURE.

WALT HANDELSMAN
Courtesy Times-Picayune (N.O.)

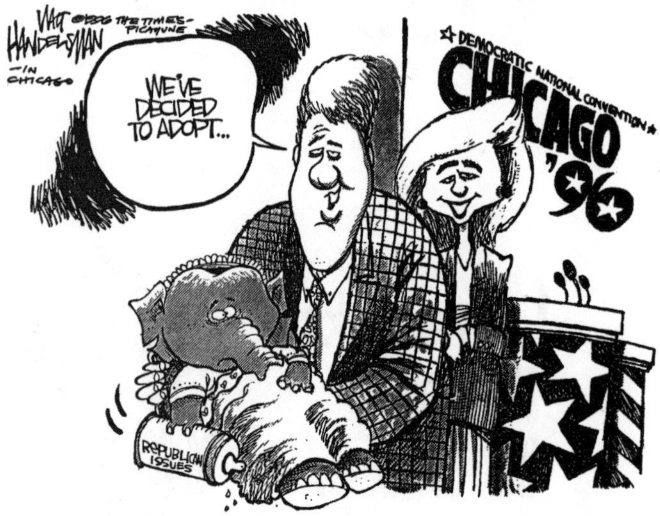
WALT HANDELSMAN ©1996 THE TIMES-PICAYUNE —IN CHICAGO
WE'VE DECIDED TO ADOPT...
DEMOCRATIC NATIONAL CONVENTION
CHICAGO '96
REPUBLICAN ISSUES

CLAY JONES
Courtesy Mississippi Business Journal

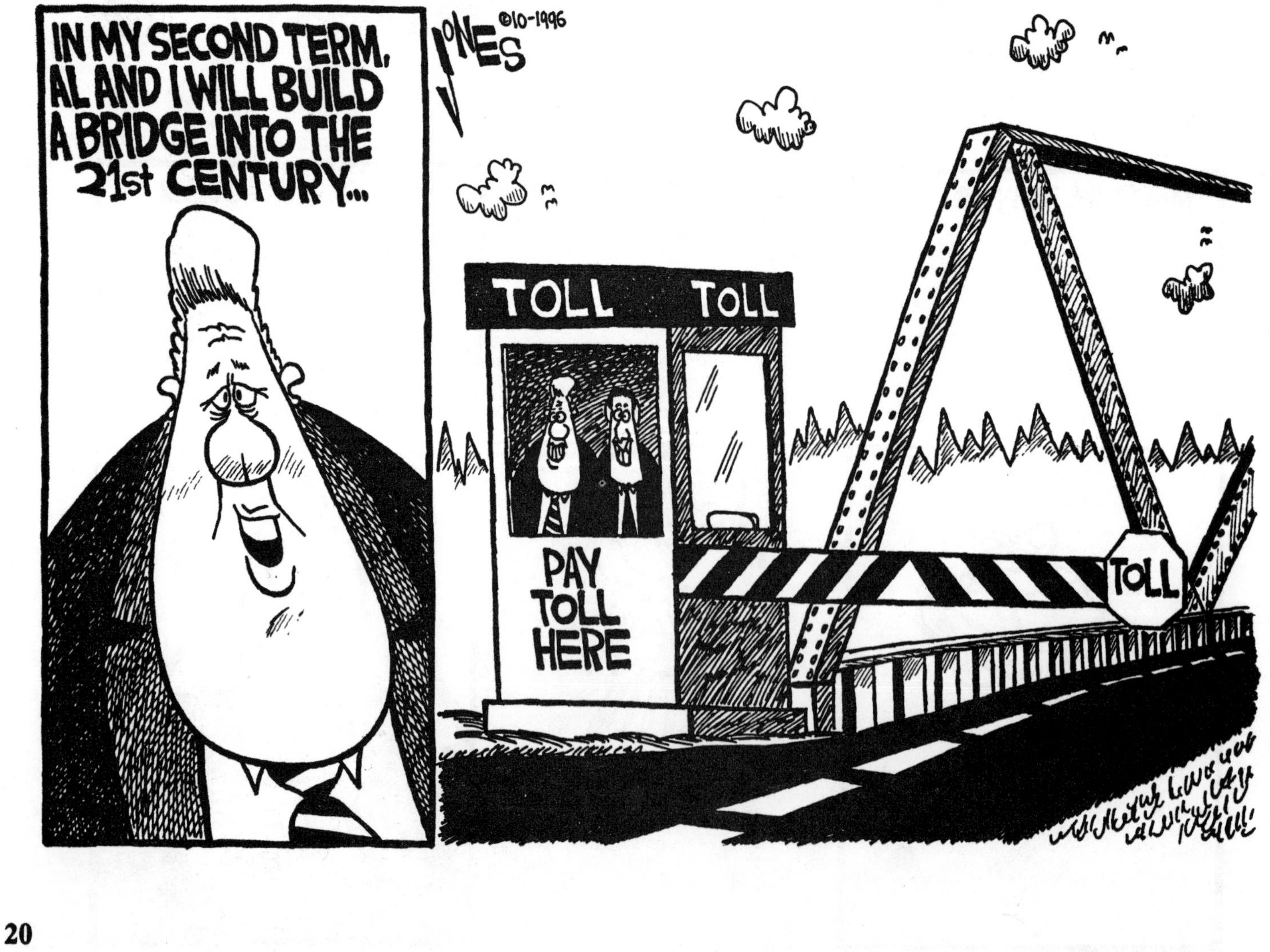
IN MY SECOND TERM, AL AND I WILL BUILD A BRIDGE INTO THE 21st CENTURY...
JONES ©10-1996
TOLL TOLL
PAY TOLL HERE
TOLL

STEVEN LAIT
Courtesy Oakland Tribune

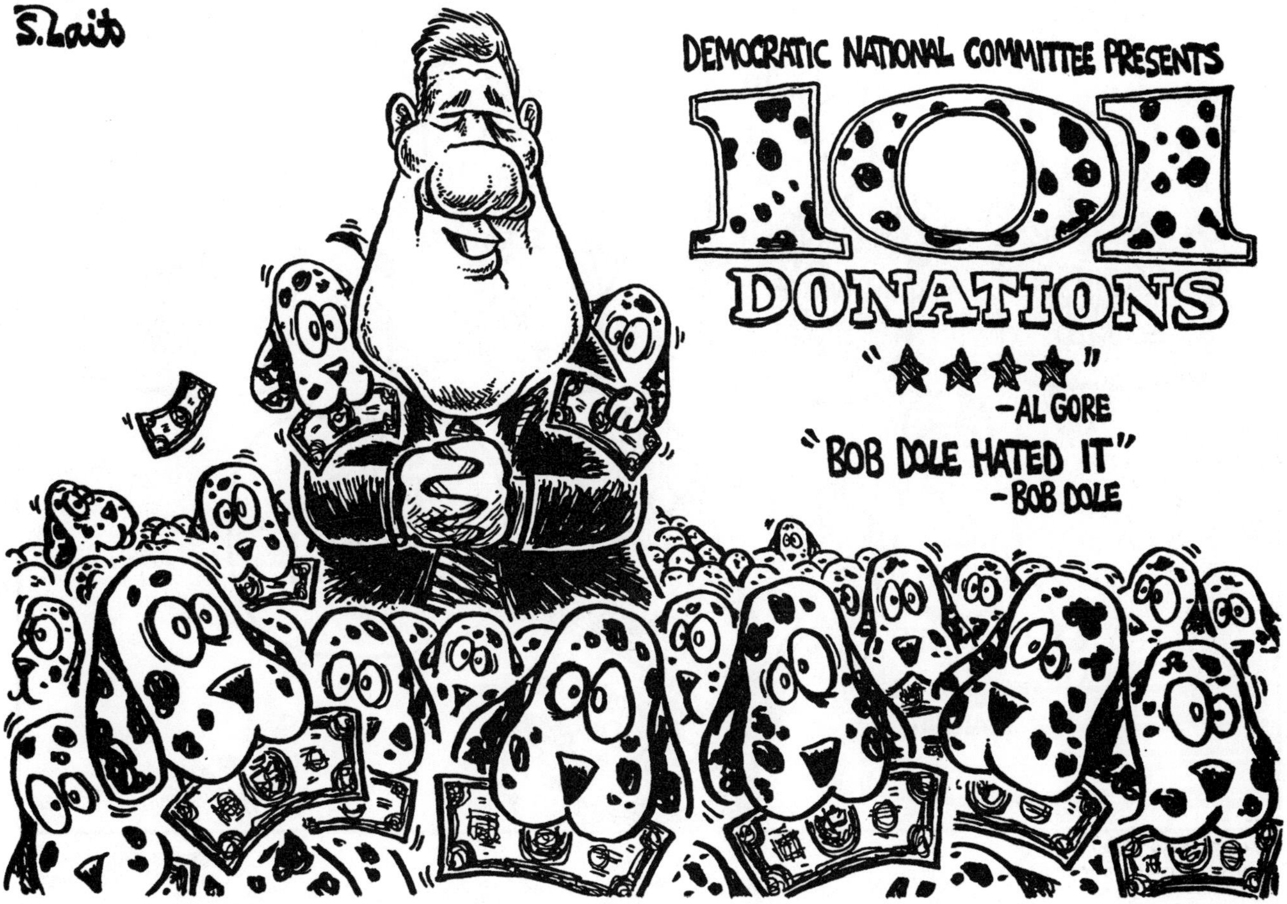
S. Lait
DEMOCRATIC NATIONAL COMMITTEE PRESENTS
101
DONATIONS
"★★★★"
-AL GORE
"BOB DOLE HATED IT"
-BOB DOLE

MARK STREETER
Courtesy Savannah Morning News

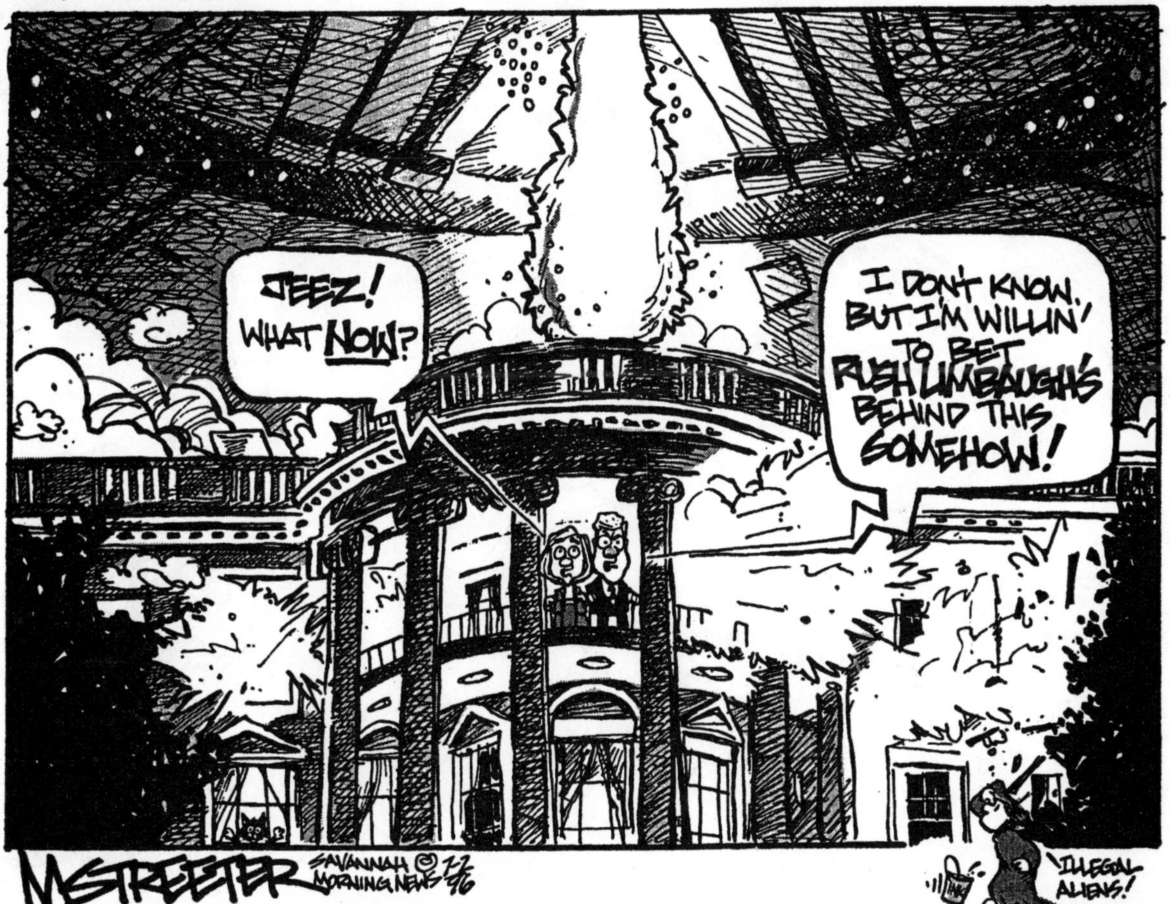
JEEZ! WHAT NOW?
I DON'T KNOW, BUT I'M WILLIN' TO BET RUSH LIMBAUGH'S BEHIND THIS SOMEHOW!
ILLEGAL ALIENS!
M STREETER SAVANNAH MORNING NEWS © 7-2-96

DICK WRIGHT
Courtesy Columbus Dispatch

DICK LOCHER
Courtesy Chicago Tribune

SVEN VAN ASSCHE
Courtesy Darien Times

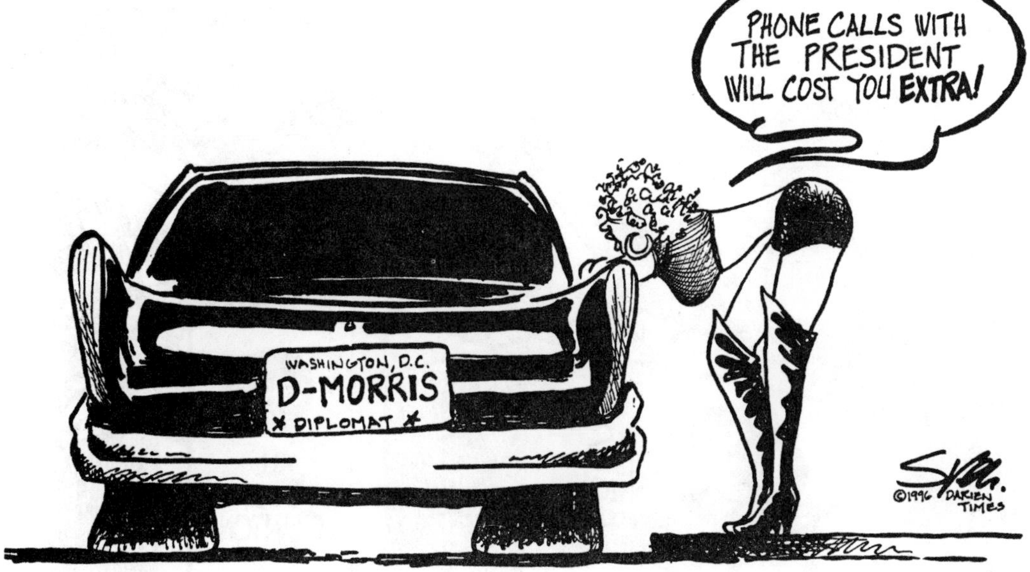
PHONE CALLS WITH THE PRESIDENT WILL COST YOU EXTRA!
WASHINGTON, D.C.
D-MORRIS
DIPLOMAT
©1996 DARIEN TIMES

J. R. ROSE
Courtesy Byrd Newspapers

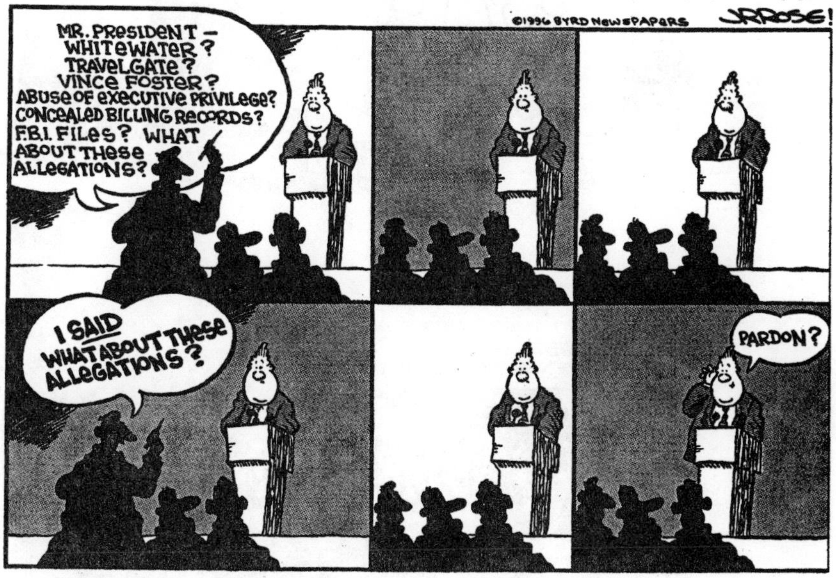
©1996 BYRD NEWSPAPERS
JRROSE!
MR. PRESIDENT – WHITEWATER? TRAVELGATE? VINCE FOSTER? ABUSE OF EXECUTIVE PRIVILEGE? CONCEALED BILLING RECORDS? F.B.I. FILES? WHAT ABOUT THESE ALLEGATIONS?
I SAID WHAT ABOUT THESE ALLEGATIONS?
PARDON?

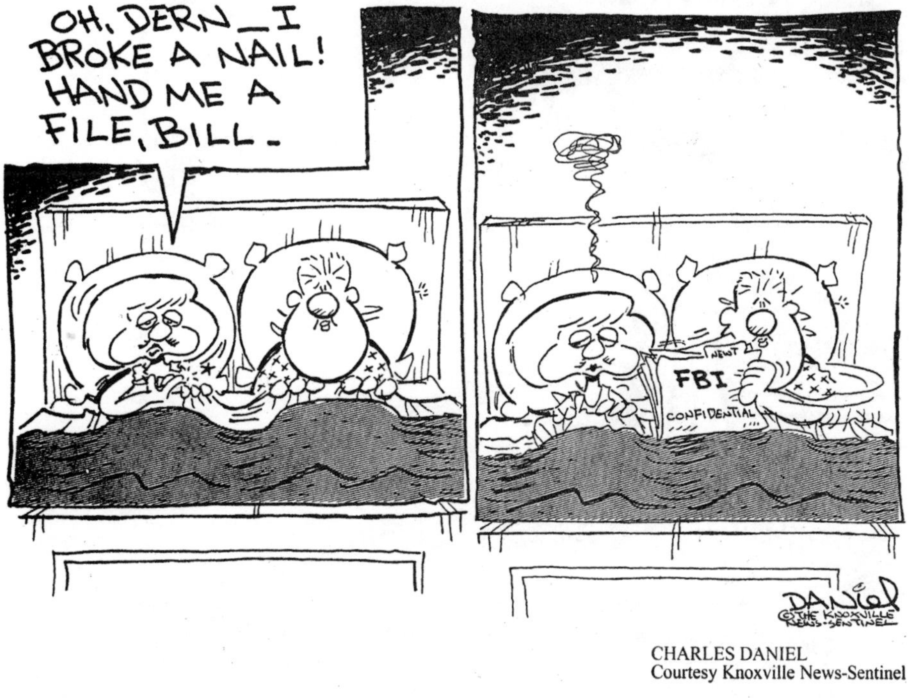
OH, DERN _ I BROKE A NAIL! HAND ME A FILE, BILL _
NEWT
FBI
CONFIDENTIAL
DANIEL
©THE KNOXVILLE NEWS-SENTINEL

CHARLES DANIEL
Courtesy Knoxville News-Sentinel

SCOTT STANTIS
Courtesy Birmingham News

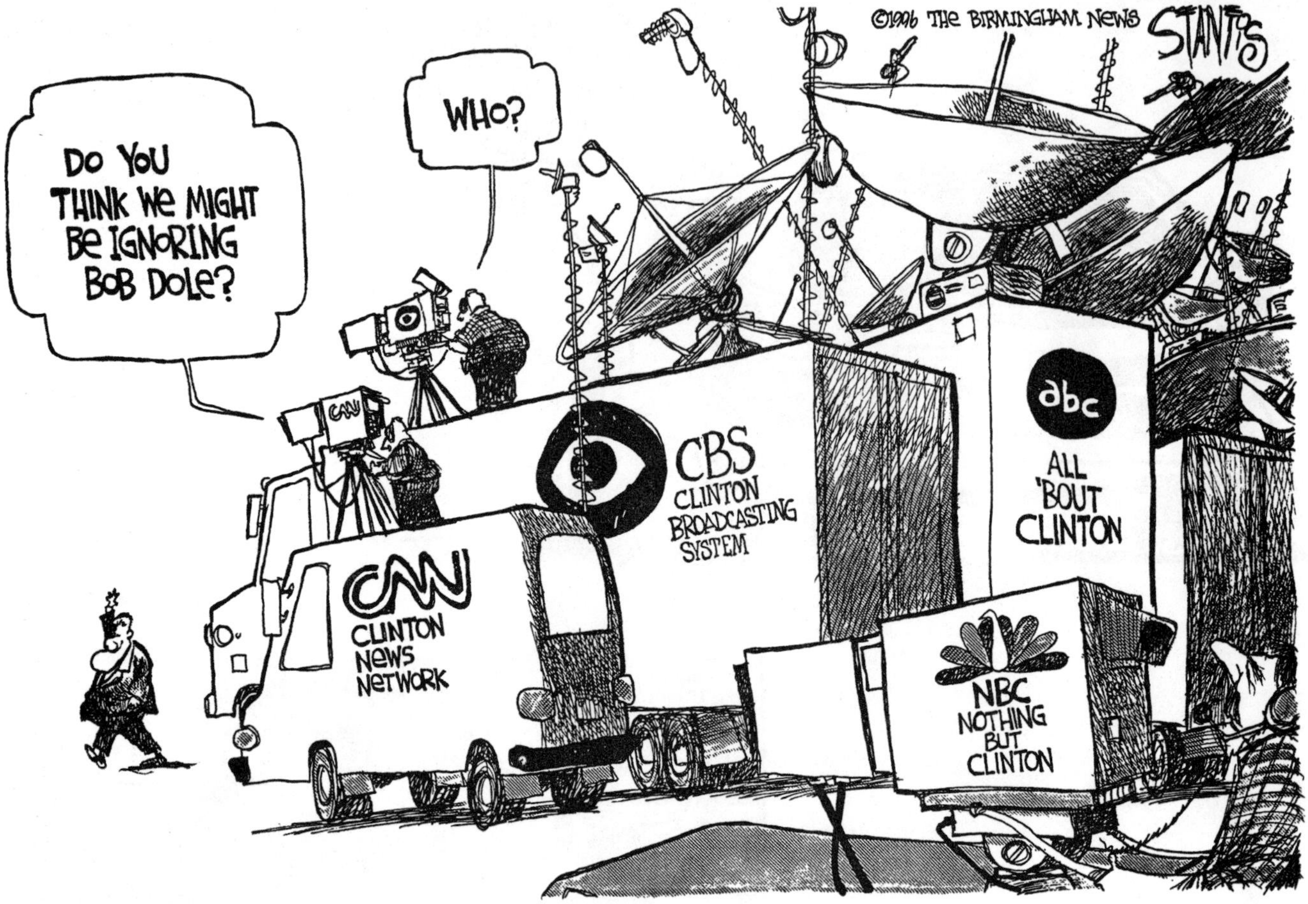
©1996 THE BIRMINGHAM NEWS
STANTIS
DO YOU THINK WE MIGHT BE IGNORING BOB DOLE?
WHO?
CNN
CLINTON NEWS NETWORK
CBS
CLINTON BROADCASTING SYSTEM
abc
ALL 'BOUT CLINTON
NBC
NOTHING BUT CLINTON

CHAN LOWE
Courtesy The News/Sun-Sentinel (Fla.)

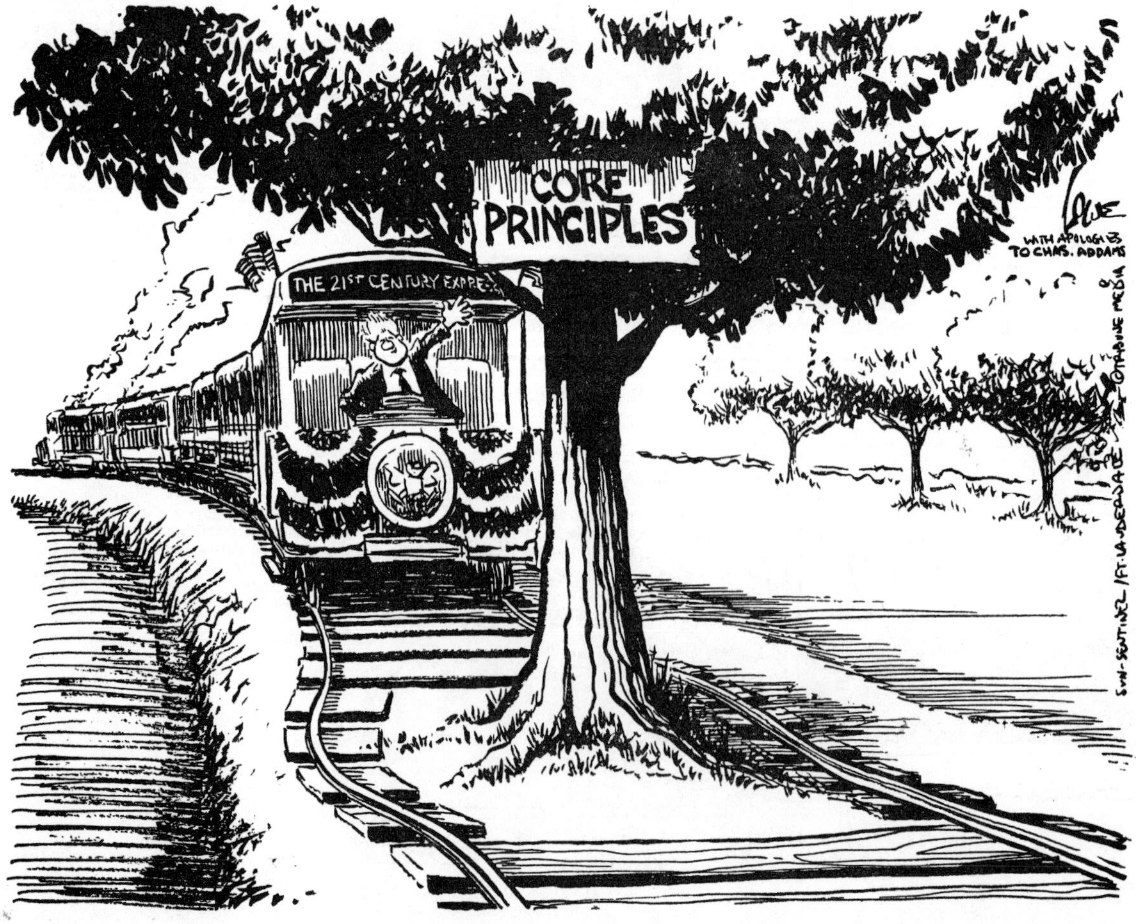
CORE PRINCIPLES
THE 21ST CENTURY EXPRE
LOWE
WITH APOLOGIES TO CHAS. ADDAMS

KIRK WALTERS
Courtesy Toledo Blade

RICK KOLLINGER
Courtesy Easton Star Democrat (Md.)

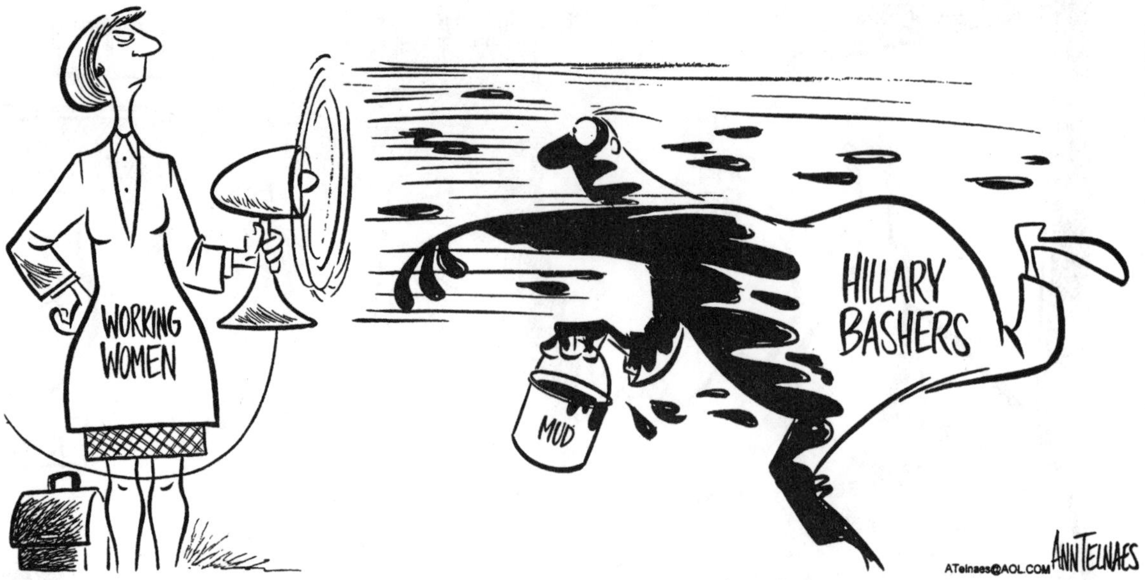
WORKING WOMEN
HILLARY BASHERS
MUD
ATelnaes@AOL.COM ANN TELNAES

ANN TELNAES
Courtesy North America Syndicate

GARY BROOKINS
Courtesy Richmond Times-Dispatch

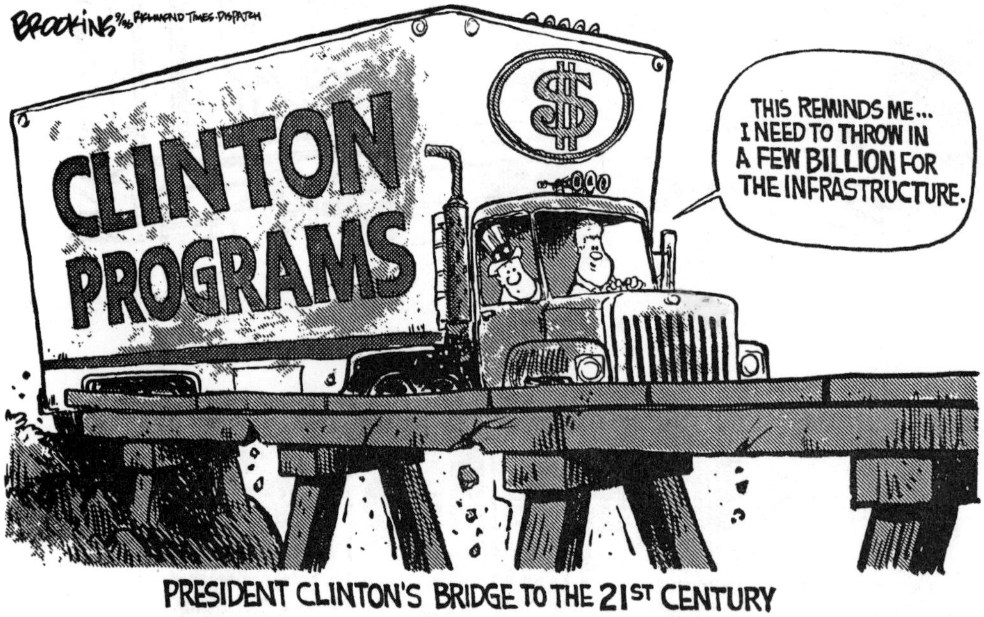
BROOKINS 9/96 RICHMOND TIMES-DISPATCH
CLINTON PROGRAMS
$
THIS REMINDS ME... I NEED TO THROW IN A FEW BILLION FOR THE INFRASTRUCTURE.
PRESIDENT CLINTON'S BRIDGE TO THE 21ST CENTURY

JERRY HOLBERT
Courtesy Boston Herald

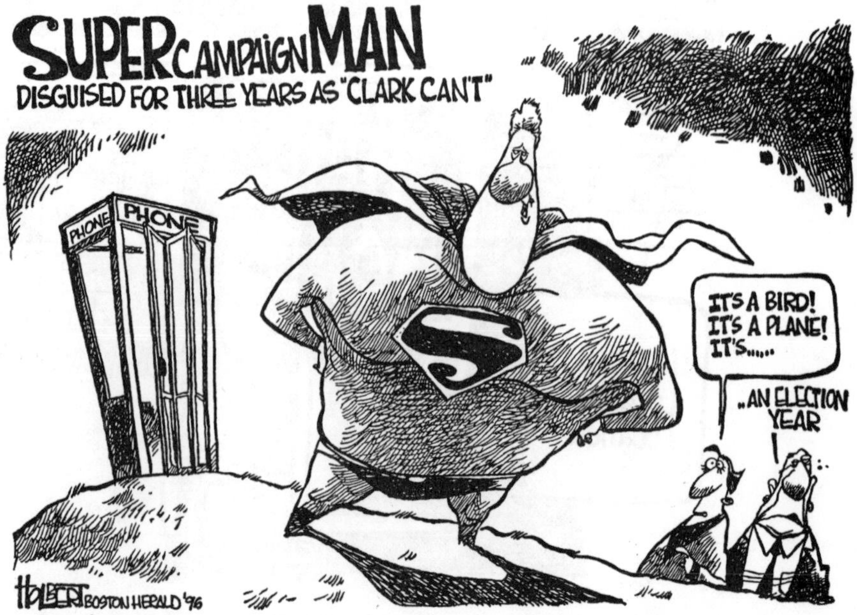
SUPER CAMPAIGN MAN
DISGUISED FOR THREE YEARS AS "CLARK CAN'T"
PHONE
PHONE
IT'S A BIRD! IT'S A PLANE! IT'S......
..AN ELECTION YEAR
HOLBERT BOSTON HERALD '96

VIC HARVILLE
Courtesy Arkansas Democrat-Gazette

GARY MCCOY
Courtesy Suburban Journals

MIKE LUCKOVICH
Courtesy Atlanta Constitution

MIKE THOMPSON
Courtesy State Journal-Register (Ill.)

DALE STEPHANOS
Courtesy Boston Herald

JOHN TREVER
Courtesy Albuquerque Journal

BOB ENGLEHART
Courtesy Hartford Courant

ETTA HULME
Courtesy Ft. Worth Star-Telegram

BOB ENGLEHART
Courtesy Hartford Courant

JIMMY MARGULIES
Courtesy The Record (N.J.)/
North America Syndicate (by permission)

"We're running low on confetti, Hillary... go shred some more files."

DALE STEPHANOS
Courtesy Boston Herald

WATERGATE 1974

WHITEWATER 1996

BOB GORRELL
Courtesy Richmond Times-Dispatch

DOUG MACGREGOR
Courtesy Ft. Meyers News-Press

JACK HIGGINS
Courtesy Chicago Sun-Times

THE BEST LITTLE WHITE HOUSE IN WASHINGTON...

MIKE PETERS
Courtesy Dayton Daily News

JAKE FULLER
Courtesy Gainesville Sun

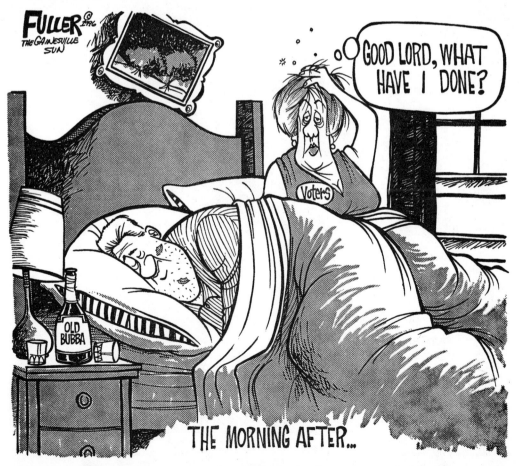

33

Berry's World

101 ALLEGATIONS

© 1996 by NEA, Inc.

JIM BERRY
Courtesy NEA

JOHN KNUDSEN
Courtesy St. Louis Review

FIRSTS

JIM LANGE
Courtesy Daily Oklahoman

ROB ROGERS
Courtesy Pittsburgh Post-Gazette

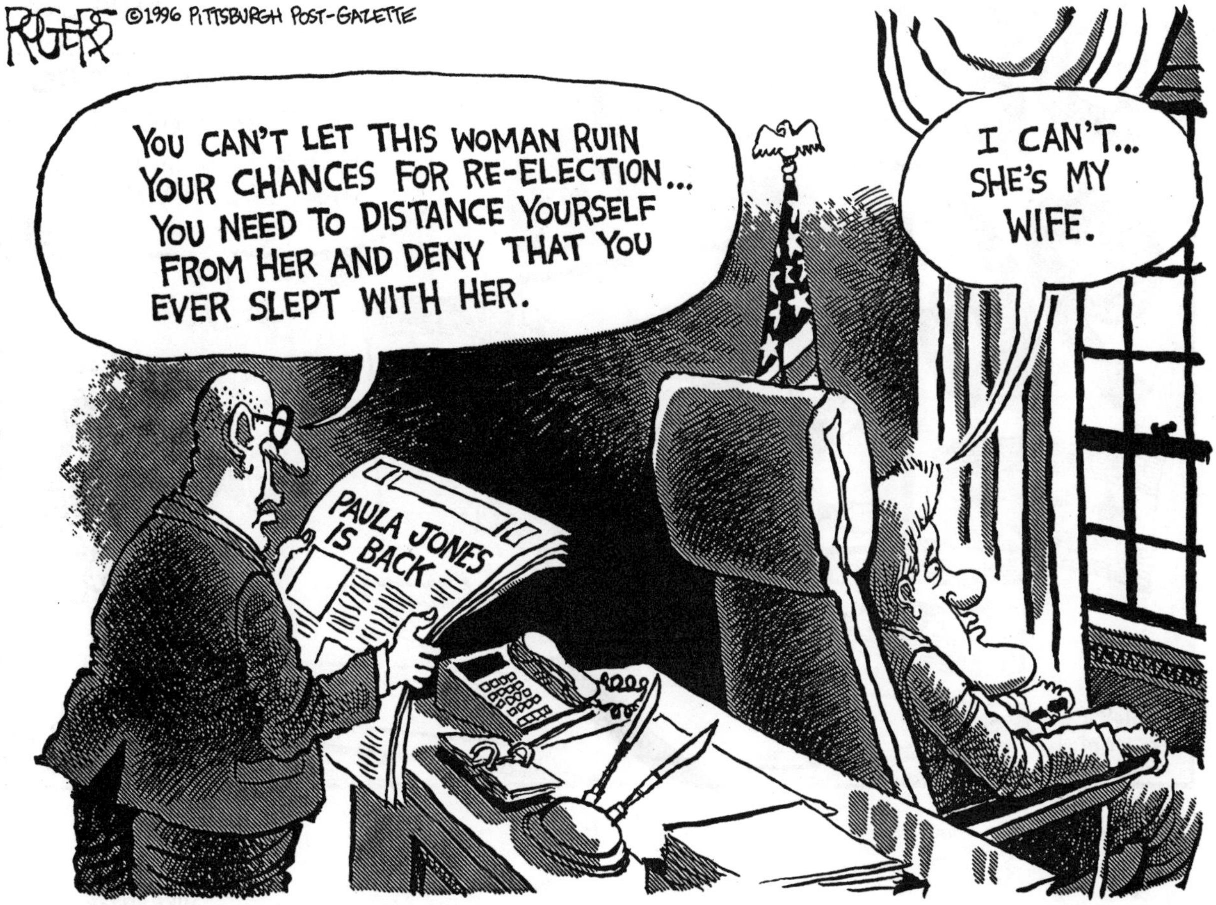
ROGERS ©1996 PITTSBURGH POST-GAZETTE
YOU CAN'T LET THIS WOMAN RUIN YOUR CHANCES FOR RE-ELECTION... YOU NEED TO DISTANCE YOURSELF FROM HER AND DENY THAT YOU EVER SLEPT WITH HER.
PAULA JONES IS BACK
I CAN'T... SHE'S MY WIFE.

MIKE PETERS
Courtesy Dayton Daily News

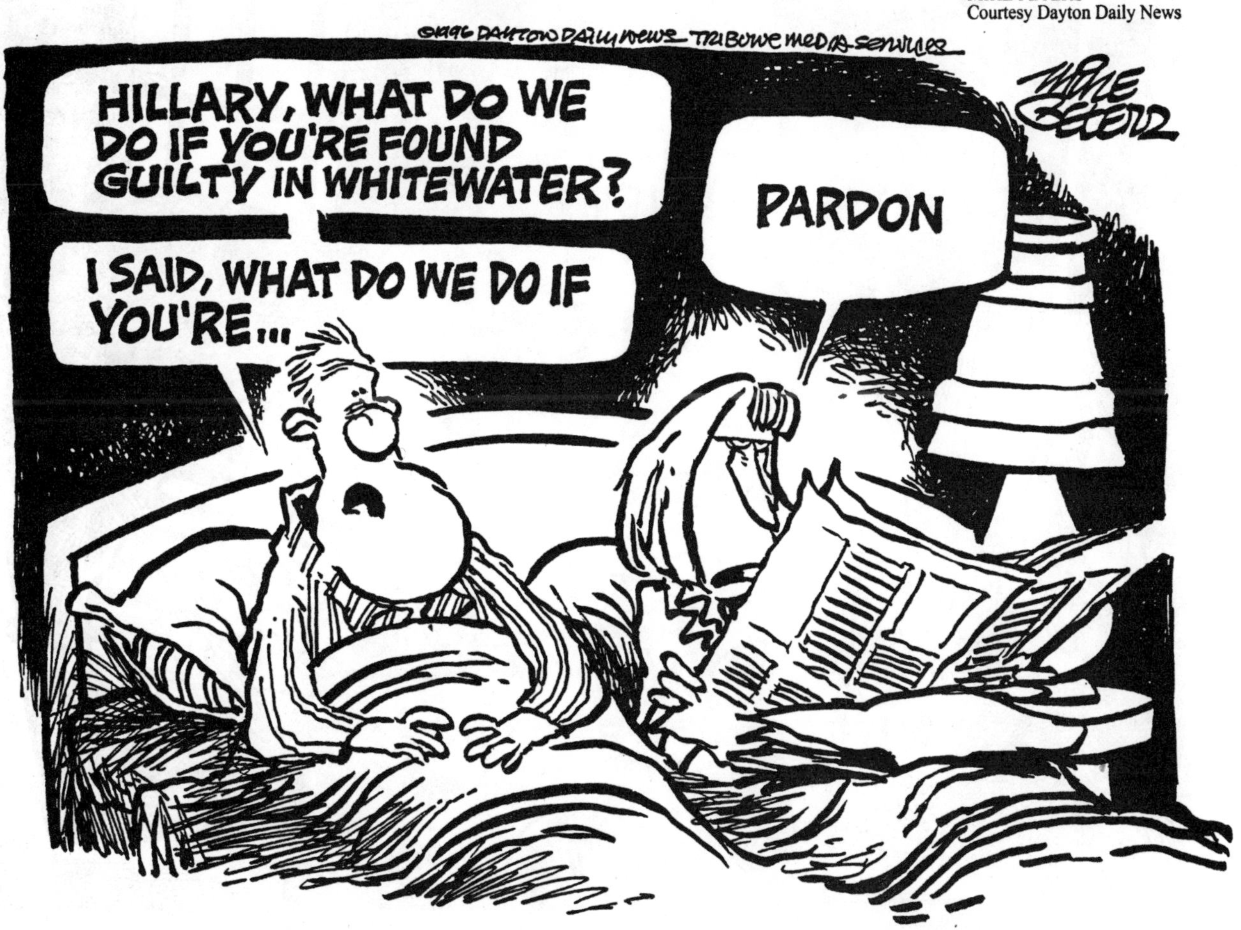
HILLARY, WHAT DO WE DO IF YOU'RE FOUND GUILTY IN WHITEWATER?
I SAID, WHAT DO WE DO IF YOU'RE...
PARDON
MIKE PETERS

ED STEIN
Courtesy Rocky Mountain News and NEA

MIKE RITTER
Courtesy Tribune Newspapers

REX BABIN
Courtesy Albany Times Union

WAYNE STAYSKAL
Courtesy Tampa Tribune

"THE CAMPAIGN IS OVER. WE CAN TURN THE FIRST LADY LOOSE."

MIKE RITTER
Courtesy Tribune Newspapers

CHRIS OBRION
Courtesy Free Lance-Star (Va.)

DENNIS DRAUGHON
Courtesy Scranton Times

SCOTT STANTIS
Courtesy Birmingham News

The Dole Campaign

From the outset, the Dole campaign for president had trouble getting out of the starting blocks. In January President Clinton's State of the Union address received high marks from political observers, while Bob Dole's response was generally characterized as "dour." That seemed to set the tone for the campaign.

Dole set a precedent by resigning from the Senate in order to devote time to his campaign. At the convention the Republican standard-bearer called for a plank in the platform stating that although the party was pro-life, it respected the views of party members who favor abortion.

Jack Kemp was chosen as Dole's running mate, and former Gen. Colin Powell delivered a well-received speech at the convention. Challenger Dole doggedly pushed his proposal for a 15 percent tax cut, but polls failed to show much improvement in his standing.

Throughout the campaign, Republicans hammered away at Clinton's character, but to the voters it was a non-issue. They seemed to feel that since Clinton had clearly moved to the middle on most political issues, Dole was merely responding "Me, too."

SCOTT WILLIS
Courtesy San Jose Mercury

DOUG MACGREGOR
Courtesy Ft. Meyers News-Press

ABORTION ISSUE

BUBBA FLINT
Courtesy Arlington Morning News

JOE MAJESKI
Courtesy The Times-Leader (Pa.)

"ACTUALLY, BOB, YOU ARE A BRIDGE TO THE FUTURE..."

DAVID DONAR
Courtesy Macomb Daily (Miss.)

JIM BORGMAN
Courtesy Cincinnati Enquirer

MICHAEL RAMIREZ
Courtesy Memphis Commercial Appeal

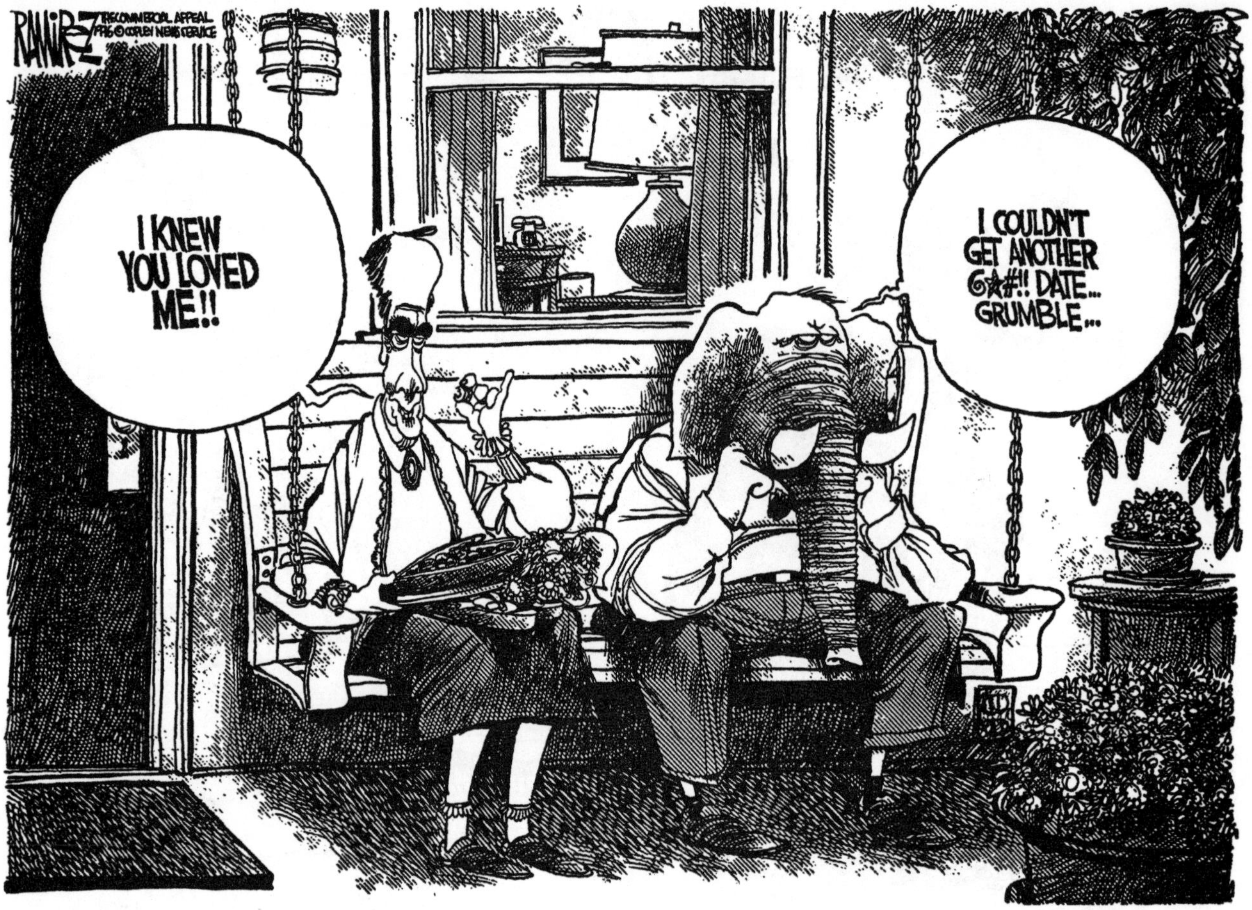

RAMIREZ
I KNEW YOU LOVED ME!!
I COULDN'T GET ANOTHER G@#!! DATE... GRUMBLE...

MIKE PETERS
Courtesy Dayton Daily News

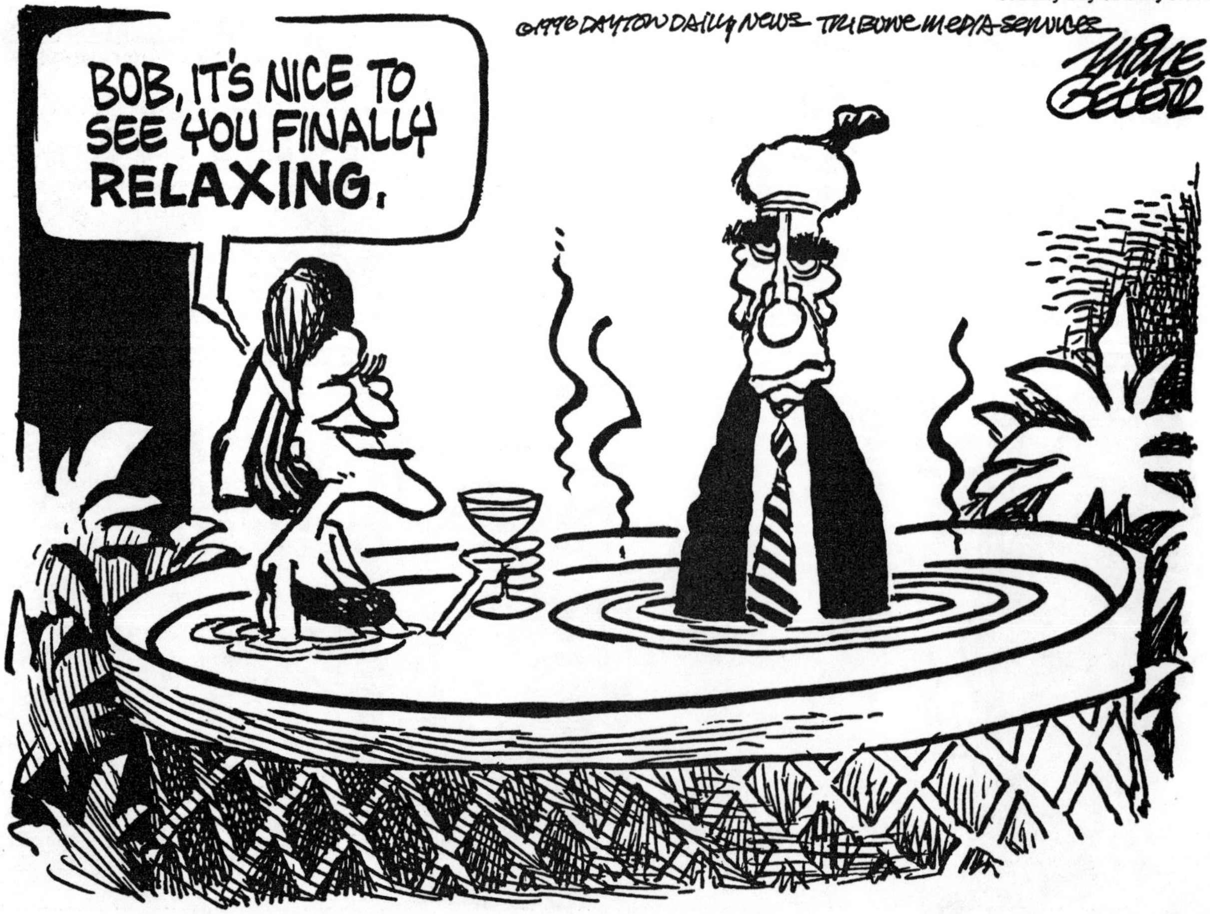

©1996 DAYTON DAILY NEWS - TRIBUNE MEDIA SERVICES
MIKE PETERS
BOB, IT'S NICE TO SEE YOU FINALLY **RELAXING**.

PAUL CONRAD
Courtesy L.A. Times Syndicate

THOMAS BOLDT
Courtesy Calgary Herald

Berry's World

JIM BERRY
Courtesy NEA

ERIC SMITH
Courtesy Capital Gazette Newspapers

BILL WHITEHEAD
Courtesy Kansas City Business Journal

ANN TELNAES
Courtesy North America Syndicate

JOHN DEERING
Courtesy Arkansas Democrat-Gazette

MIKE RITTER
Courtesy Tribune Newspapers

47

BILL GARNER
Courtesy Washington Times

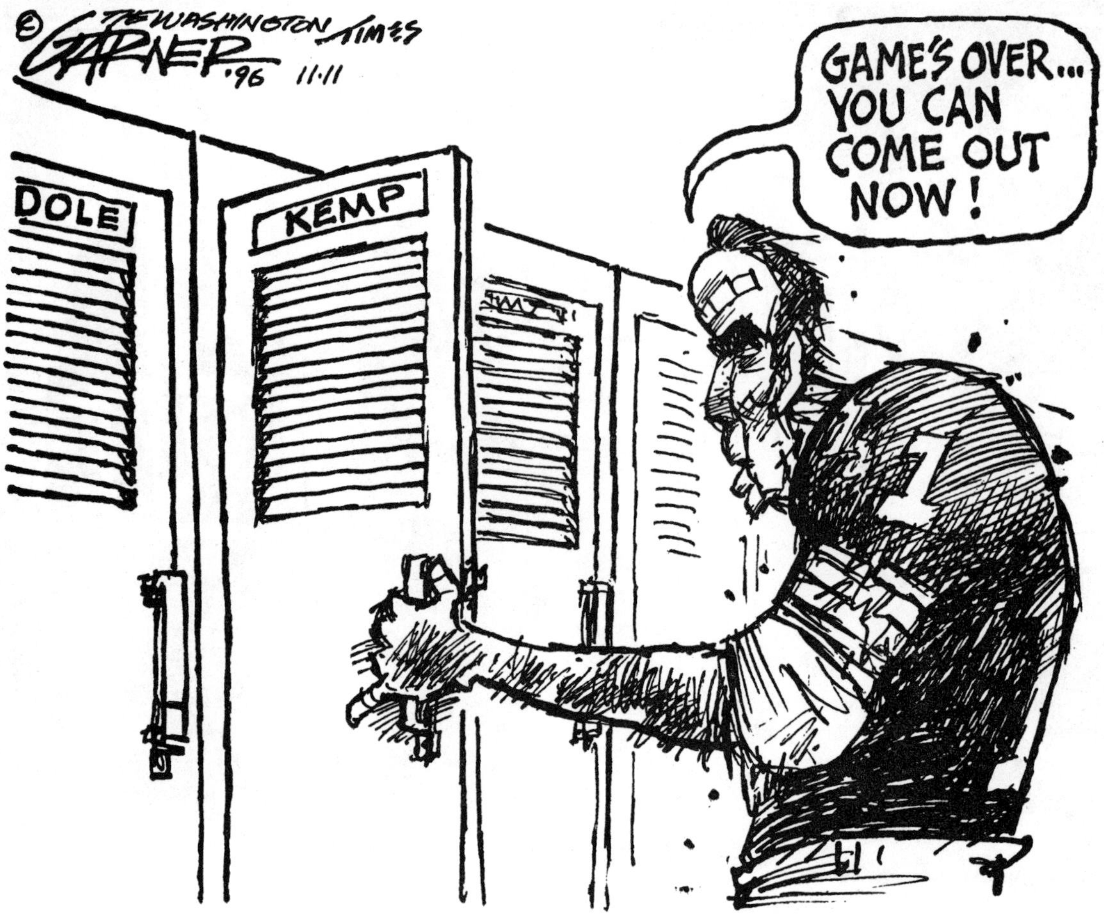
© THE WASHINGTON TIMES GARNER '96 11·11
DOLE
KEMP
GAME'S OVER... YOU CAN COME OUT NOW!

JIM MCCLOSKEY
Courtesy Staunton Daily News Leader

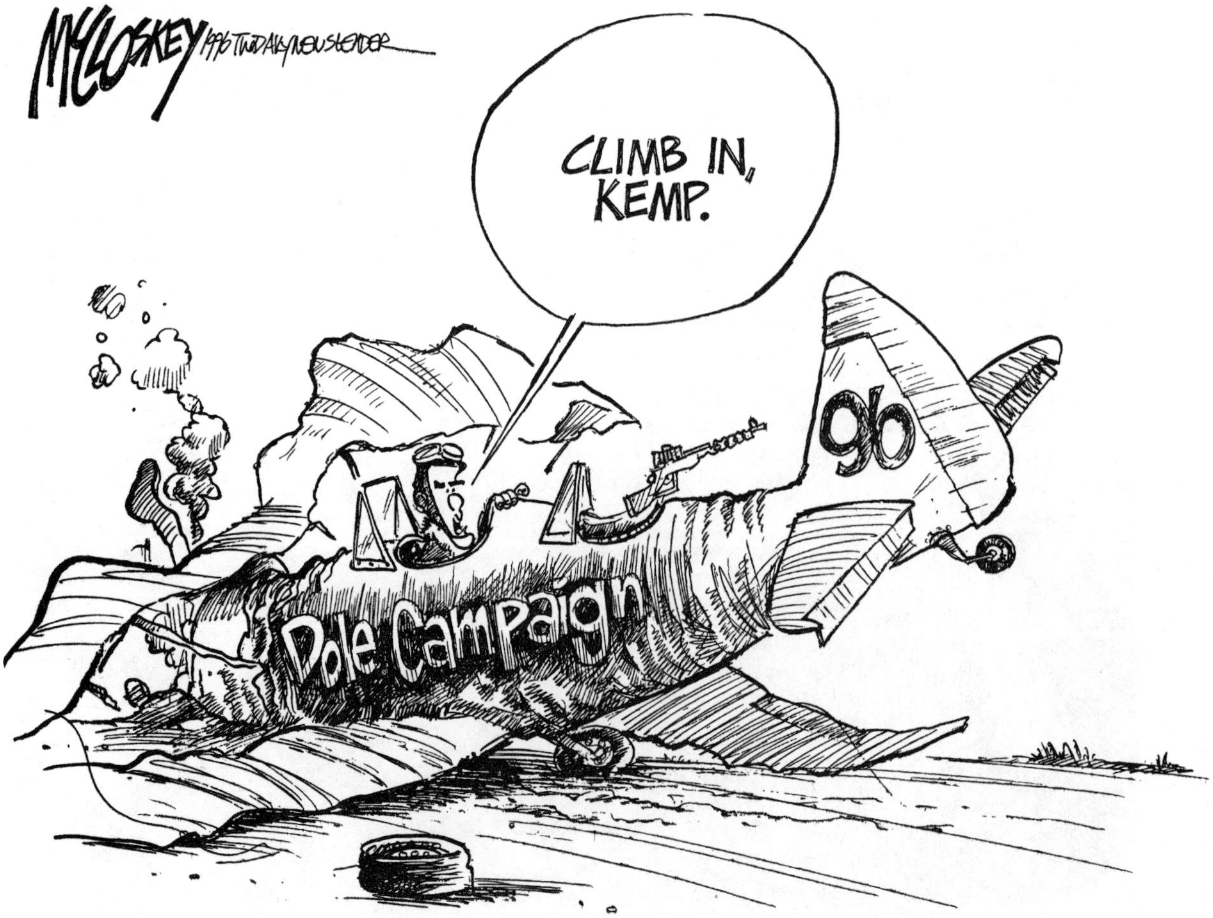
CLIMB IN, KEMP.
96
Dole Campaign

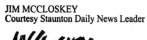

Berry's World

"NOT NOW!"

JIM BERRY
Courtesy NEA

TOM BECK
Courtesy Freeport Journal-Standard (Ill.)

MILT PRIGGEE
Courtesy Spokane Spokesman-Review

DOLE'S DÉJÀ VU, ALL OVER AGAIN

1876
Bob Dole discusses strategy with General Custer

RANDY BISH
Courtesy Tribune-Review (Pa.)

CHRIS OBRION
Courtesy Free Lance-Star (Va.)

GEORGE DANBY
Courtesy Bangor Daily News

Ross Perot

To the surprise of no one, Ross Perot won the nomination of his Reform Party for president of the United States, beating out former Colorado Gov. Richard Lamm by a two-to-one margin.

This time around Perot accepted contributions and chose to make use of matching government funds instead of financing his own campaign. During his 1992 bid for the presidency Perot spent nearly $60 million of his own money.

Lamm refused to endorse Perot, apparently upset by the way the nominating process was handled.

Perot was denied a national forum in the televised presidential debates after it was decided that his 5 percent showing in the polls did not qualify him as a serious candidate. President Clinton said Perot should be included, but Republican candidate Bob Dole disagreed.

In the presidential election, Perot won 8 percent of the vote, less than half of what he pulled in 1992.

JACK OHMAN
Courtesy Portland Oregonian

STEVE KELLEY
Courtesy San Diego Union

PAUL SZEP
Courtesy Boston Globe

PASSING THE TORCH

WALT HANDELSMAN
Courtesy Times-Picayune (N.O.)

LINDA BOILEAU
Courtesy Frankfort State Journal

DRAPER HILL
Courtesy Detroit News

MILT PRIGGEE
Courtesy Spokane Spokesman-Review

THE DODO BIRD COMETH

53

JOE HELLER
Courtesy Green Bay Press-Gazette

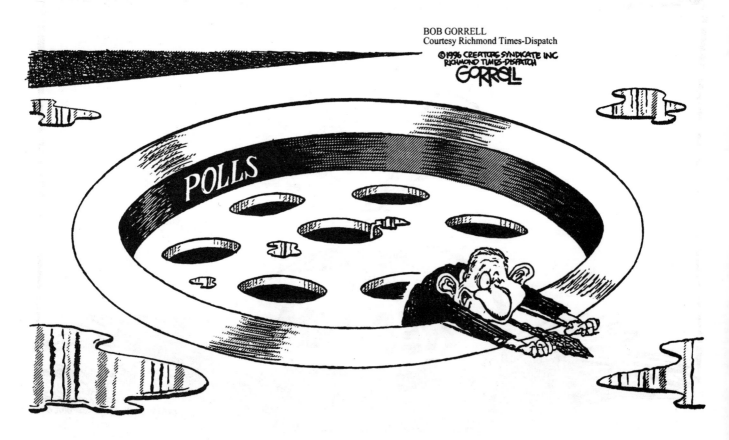

BOB GORRELL
Courtesy Richmond Times-Dispatch

"WAIT JUST ONE COTTON-PICKIN' MINUTE! . . . WHAT'S THAT GIANT SUCKING SOUND?!"

JEFF MACNELLY
Courtesy Chicago Tribune and
Tribune Media Services

DICK LOCHER
Courtesy Chicago Tribune

As the presidential candidates finally meet face-to-face a hush falls over the nation ....

Politics

Early in the election year, Republicans felt things were going their way. President Clinton's liberalism had been rejected by voters in the 1994 congressional elections, and it was widely believed that an array of White House scandals would weigh heavily against the incumbent. But voters seemed to ignore those factors as Clinton marched toward the political center.

Republican House Speaker Newt Gingrich suffered mightily, as did newly elected Republicans, who were perceived as having been responsible for a shutdown of the government during the budget battle. Gingrich, particularly, was portrayed as an ogre who was ready to throw the poor and little children to the wolves.

Patrick Buchanan emerged as a strong contender for the G.O.P. nomination after Sen. Phil Gramm, Steve Forbes, and others dropped out. But Buchanan was too far to the right for many Republicans.

In a late-hour chat on election night, television commentator David Brinkley found himself at the center of the news. Analyzing Clinton's victory speech, Brinkley said it was "one of the worst things I've ever heard." Then he added, "He's a bore and will always be a bore." Despite the comments, Clinton later appeared on Brinkley's television show.

CLAY BENNETT
Courtesy North America Syndicate

JEFF PARKER
Courtesy Florida Today

TIM HARTMAN
Courtesy North Hills News Record (Pa.)

JACK HIGGINS
Courtesy Chicago Sun-Times

GEORGE DANBY
Courtesy Bangor Daily News

ROB ROGERS
Courtesy Pittsburgh Post-Gazette

THE GOP BIG TENT...

STEVEN LAIT
Courtesy Oakland Tribune

JIM MORIN
Courtesy Miami Herald

GLENN MCCOY
Courtesy Belleville News-Democrat (Ill.)

MARK STREETER
Courtesy Savannah Morning News

PAT BUCHANAN'S
FOREIGN AND DOMESTIC POLICIES

JACK OHMAN
Courtesy Portland Oregonian

EDGAR SOLLER
Courtesy California Examiner

FRANK CAMMUSO
Courtesy Syracuse Herald-Journal

JERRY BUCKLEY
Courtesy Express Newspapers

ERIC SMITH
Courtesy Capital Gazette Newspapers

DENNY PRITCHARD
Courtesy Ottawa Citizen

ED STEIN
Courtesy Rocky Mountain News and NEA

FRANK CAMMUSO
Courtesy Syracuse Herald-Journal

JACK OHMAN
Courtesy Portland Oregonian

JOHN MARSHALL
Courtesy Binghampton Press and Sun-Bulletin

MALCOLM MAYES
Courtesy Edmonton Journal

ROGER HARVELL
Courtesy Greenville News

JIM LANGE
Courtesy Daily Oklahoman

JACK MCLEOD
Courtesy Federal Times

MARK THORNHILL
Courtesy North County Times (Calif.)

REAL LIFE ON MARS ...

WATCHING ANOTHER SCI-FI?

YEAH. IT'S CALLED, A POLITICAL CONVENTION.

LINDA BOILEAU
Courtesy Frankfort State Journal

looks like good-news... bad-news on this election... good-news... there are two distinct choices... the bad-news the choices are dole and clinton

STEPHEN TEMPLETON
Courtesy Comic Relief/Future Features

JOHN DEROSIER
Courtesy Mobile Press Register

©1996 MOBILE PRESS REGISTER

ENTHUSIASM

CLINTON '96

DOLE '96

DRAPER HILL
Courtesy Detroit News

JACK JURDEN
Courtesy Wilmington News Journal

JACK OHMAN
Courtesy Portland Oregonian

JAMES LARRICK
Courtesy Columbus Dispatch

TOM ENGELHARDT
Courtesy St. Louis Post-Dispatch

'Of Course It's All Legal —
We Make The Laws, Don't We?'

BRIAN DUFFY
Courtesy Des Moines Register

Congress

With strong bipartisan and presidential approval, Congress passed sweeping reform of telecommunications regulations, taking into account the computer revolution. The new regulations make for freer competition between television and radio broadcasters and telephone companies.

After much bickering and two government shutdowns, Congress finally passed a budget package in late April, and President Clinton signed it. A bitter battle raged between the two parties over a move to raise the minimum wage. Republicans opposed the hike, contending it would hurt business and cause unemployment among the lowest-paid workers. Eventually the minimum wage was increased to $5.15 an hour.

Just prior to Bob Dole's leaving the Senate for the campaign trail, he again brought a balanced budget amendment to the floor. It was defeated, two votes shy of the required two-thirds majority. The vote put President Clinton, who opposed the measure, at odds with the vast majority of Americans.

Congress continued to drag its heels on medicare, campaign finance reform, term limits, and the curbing of special interests.

REX BABIN
Courtesy Albany Times Union

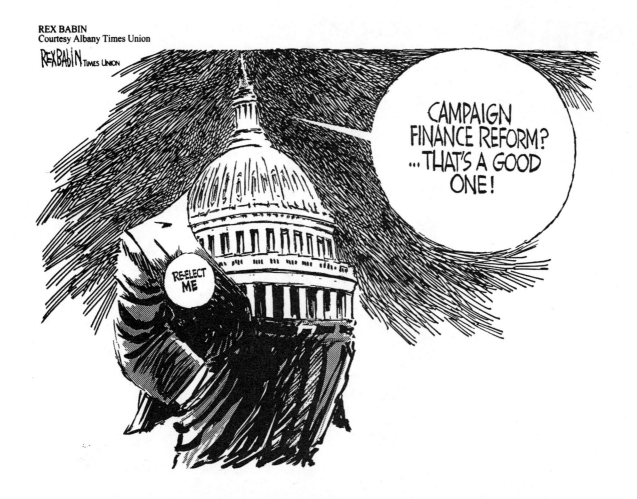

73

JOE LONG
Courtesy Little Falls Evening Times (N.Y.)

JAMES MERCADO
Courtesy The Garden Island

ED STEIN
Courtesy Rocky Mountain News and NEA

PAUL CONRAD
Courtesy L.A. Times Syndicate

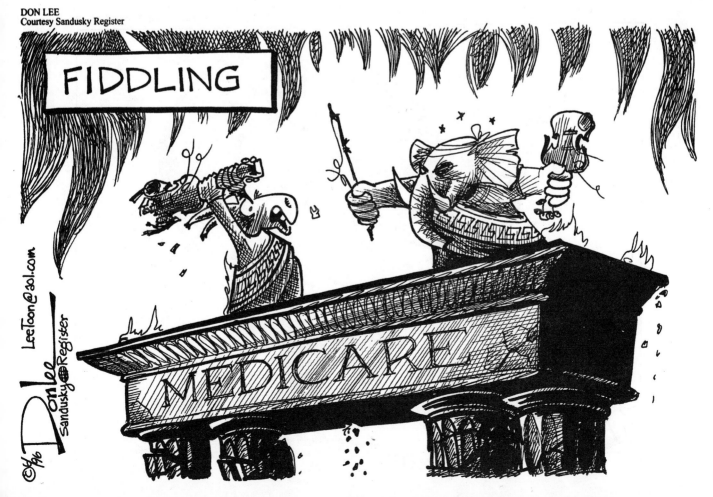

THE EVER REMARKABLE SHRINKING MAN

ART HENRIKSON
Courtesy Daily Herald (Ill.)

VIC CANTONE
Courtesy King Features/North America Syndicate

BEAST OF BURDEN

STEVE MCBRIDE
Courtesy Independence Daily Reporter (Kans.)

CHAN LOWE
Courtesy The News/Sun-Sentinel (Fla.)

KIRK ANDERSON
Courtesy Madison (Wis.) Capital Times

WAYNE STROOT
Courtesy Hastings Tribune

THE FREE MARKET OF IDEAS

STEVE LINDSTROM
Courtesy Duluth News-Tribune

78

STEVE MCBRIDE
Courtesy Independence Daily Reporter (Kans.)

CLAY JONES
Courtesy Mississippi Business Journal

JIM MORIN
Courtesy Miami Herald

GARY MARKSTEIN
Courtesy Milwaukee Journal Sentinel

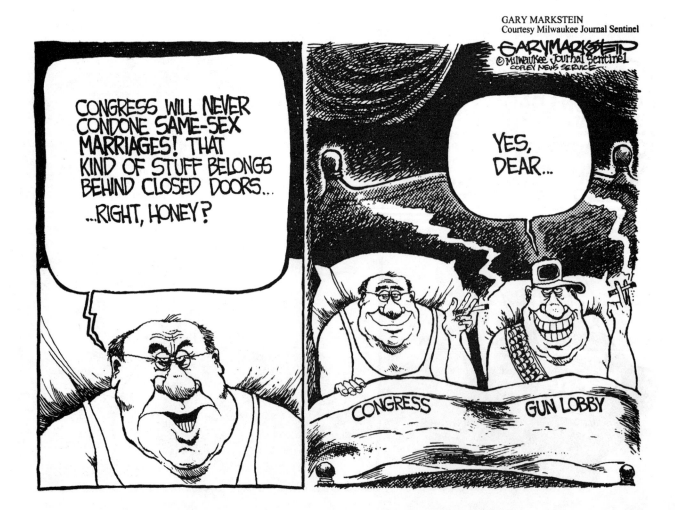

Foreign Affairs

A measure of peace broke out in some parts of the world during the year, but it was a shaky state of affairs at best. After years of bloodshed in Bosnia, the siege of Sarajevo was declared officially over.

In Israel, Likud Party leader and hardliner Benjamin Netanyahu won a slim victory over incumbent Prime Minister Shimon Peres. The government opened a tourist tunnel near a Muslim holy site, and 79 Israelis and Palestinians were killed in three days of fighting that followed.

An ailing Boris Yeltsin was re-elected president of Russia, beating back a strong challenge by Alexander Lebed, a former general who seeks to restore the old order. Iraq's Saddam Hussein attacked Kurdish rebels and defied the United Nations' no-fly zone. President Clinton responded with cruise missile attacks.

The Mad Cow Disease ravaged England, leading the government to slaughter thousands of the animals.

The U.S. was successful in blocking the re-election of Boutros Boutros-Ghali as secretary-general of the United Nations, and Britain's Prince Charles was granted a divorce from Princess Diana.

JIM MORIN
Courtesy Miami Herald

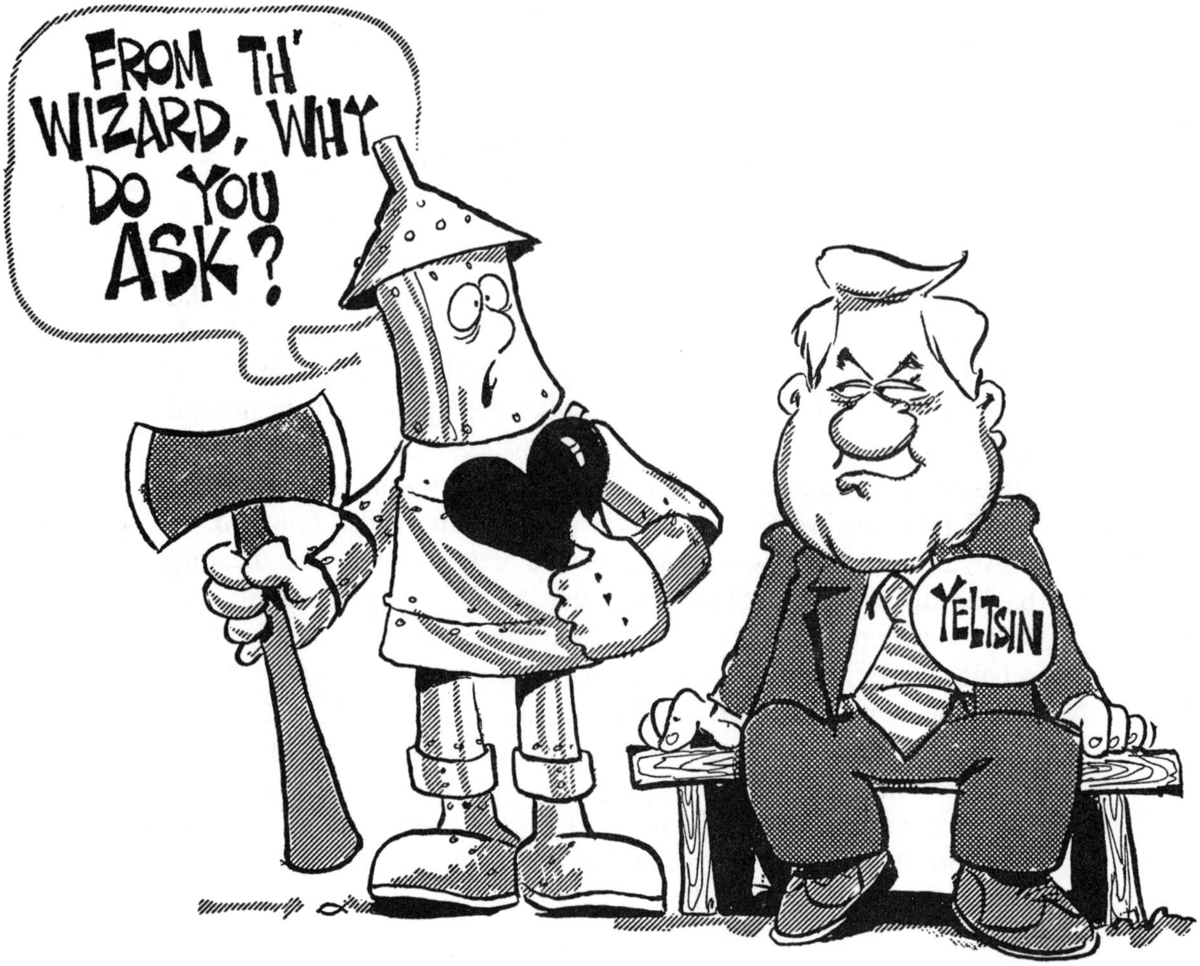
FROM TH' WIZARD, WHY DO YOU ASK?
YELTSIN

HANK MCCLURE
Courtesy Lawton Constitution

ROBERT ARIAIL
Courtesy The State (S.C.)

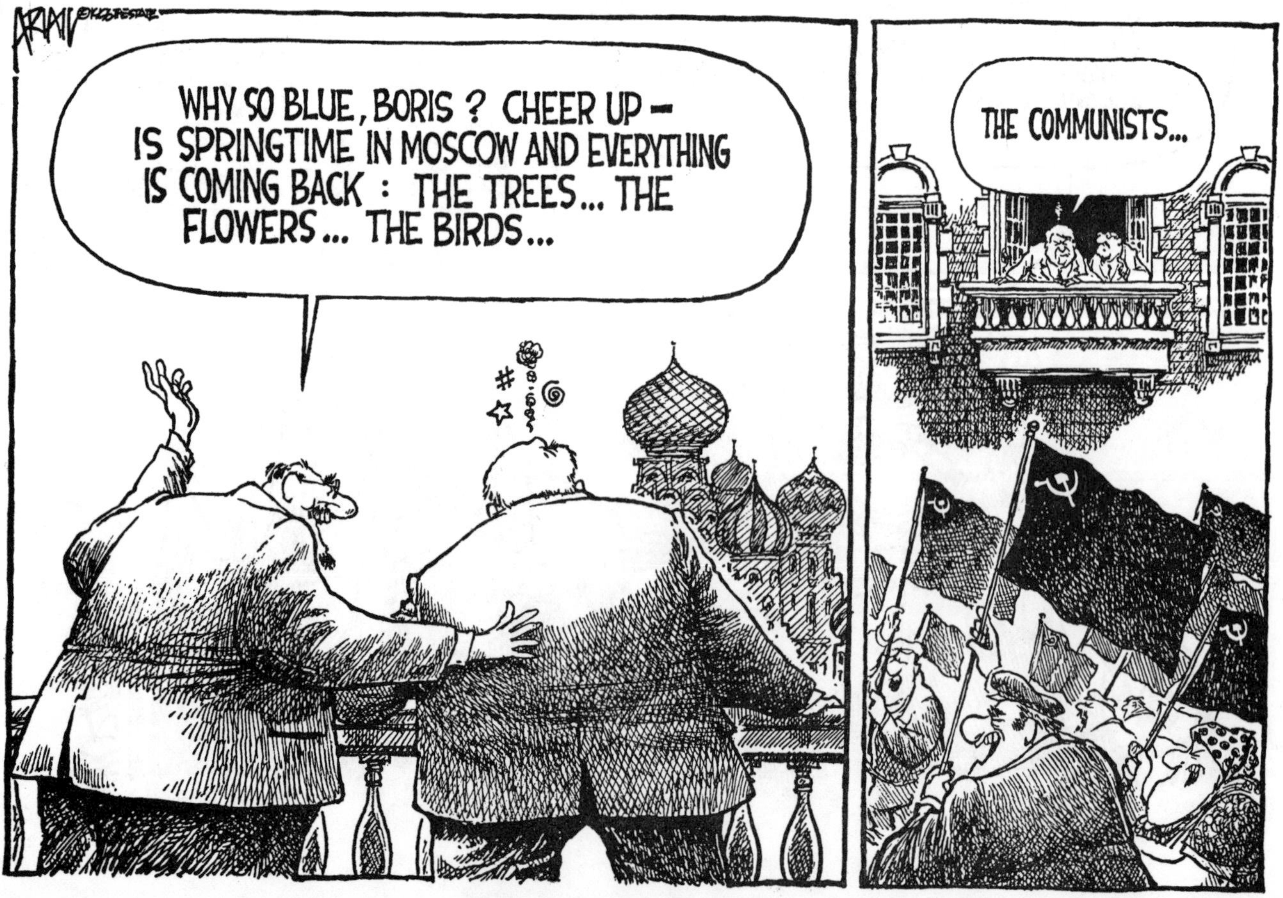
WHY SO BLUE, BORIS ? CHEER UP – IS SPRINGTIME IN MOSCOW AND EVERYTHING IS COMING BACK : THE TREES... THE FLOWERS... THE BIRDS...
THE COMMUNISTS...

BILL GARNER
Courtesy Washington Times

GARY BROOKINS
Courtesy Richmond Times-Dispatch

SANDY CAMPBELL
Courtesy The Tennessean

JEFF KOTERBA
Courtesy Omaha World-Herald

OSWALDO SAGASTEGUI
Courtesy Excelsior (Mex.)

ED GAMBLE
Courtesy Florida Times-Union

DANI AGUILA
Courtesy Filipino Reporter

LAZARO FRESQUET
Courtesy El Nuevo Herald (Miami)

86

JERRY BUCKLEY
Courtesy Express Newspapers

http://www.grimmy.com

MIKE PETERS
Courtesy Dayton Daily News

ROGER HARVELL
Courtesy Greenville News

DAVID GRANLUND
Courtesy Middlesex News

BRIAN GABLE
Courtesy Toronto Globe and Mail

JIM JORDAN
Courtesy Elmhurst Press (Ill.)

DAN MURPHY
Courtesy Vancouver Province

PAUL SZEP
Courtesy Boston Globe

HANK MCCLURE
Courtesy Lawton Constitution

JIM BERRY
Courtesy NEA

NEAL BLOOM
Courtesy Jewish Cartoon Productions

DAVID HITCH
Courtesy Worcester Telegram & Gazette

JOE MAJESKI
Courtesy The Times-Leader (Pa.)

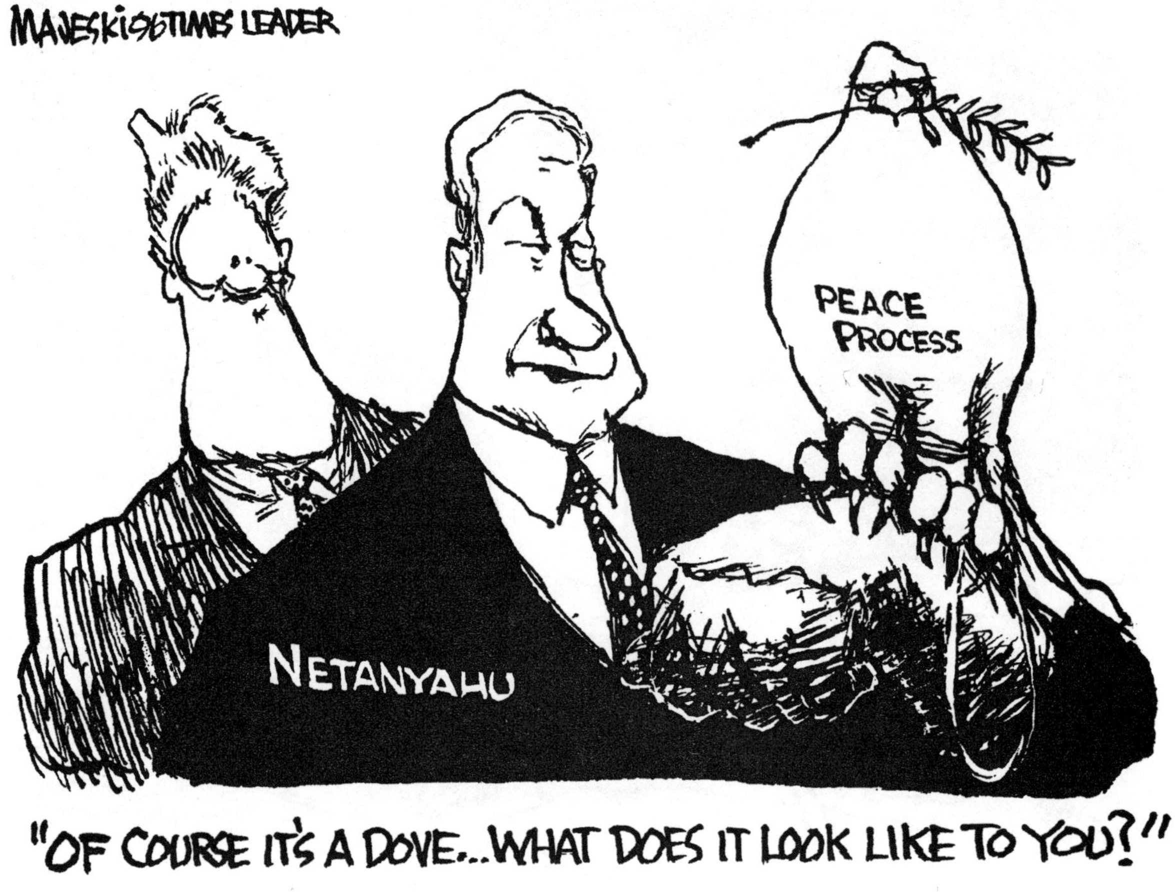
MAJESKI96TIMES LEADER
PEACE PROCESS
NETANYAHU
"OF COURSE IT'S A DOVE...WHAT DOES IT LOOK LIKE TO YOU?"

NICK ANDERSON
Courtesy Louisville Courier Journal

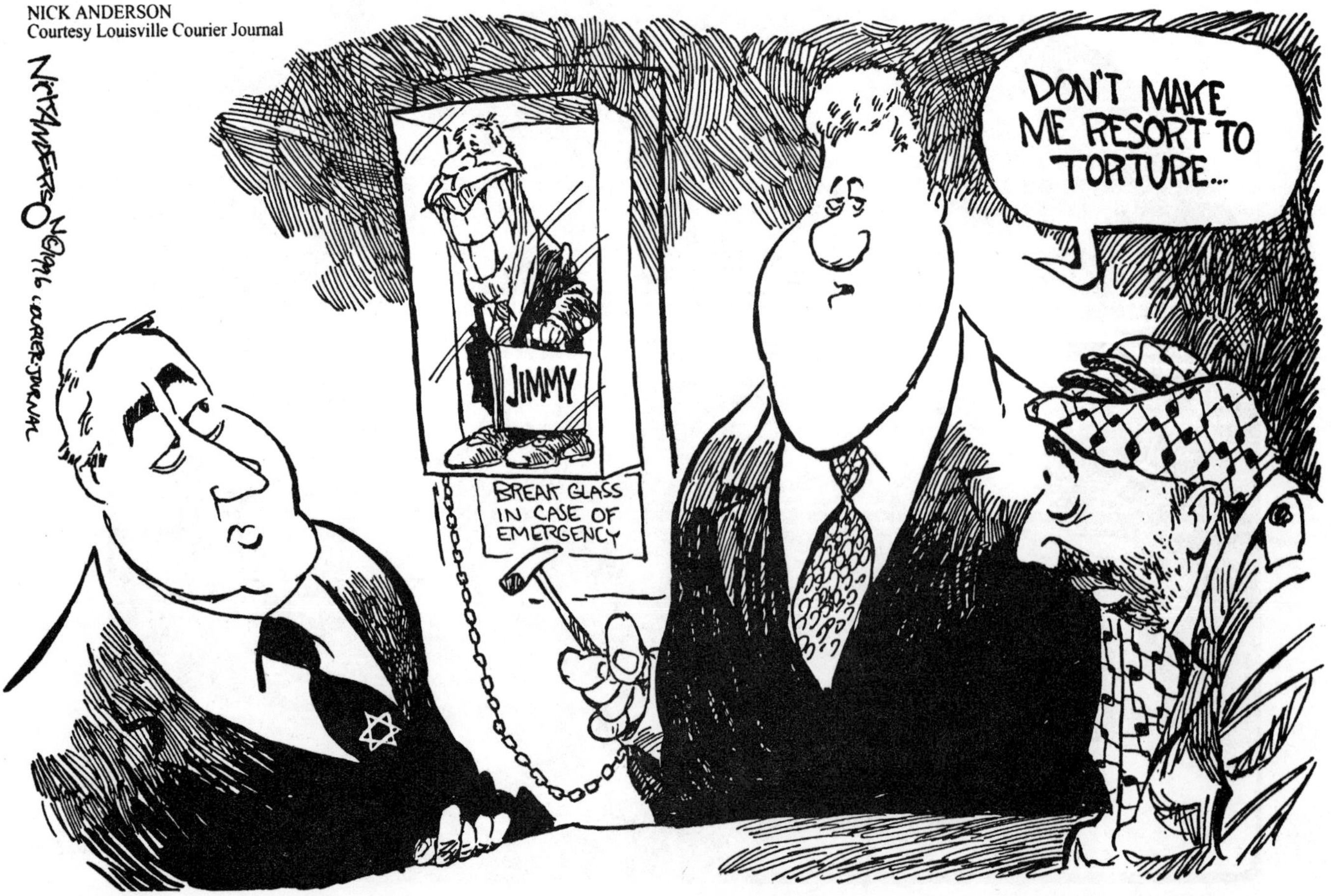
NICK ANDERSON
JIMMY
BREAK GLASS IN CASE OF EMERGENCY
DON'T MAKE ME RESORT TO TORTURE...

DANA SUMMERS
Courtesy Orlando Sentinel

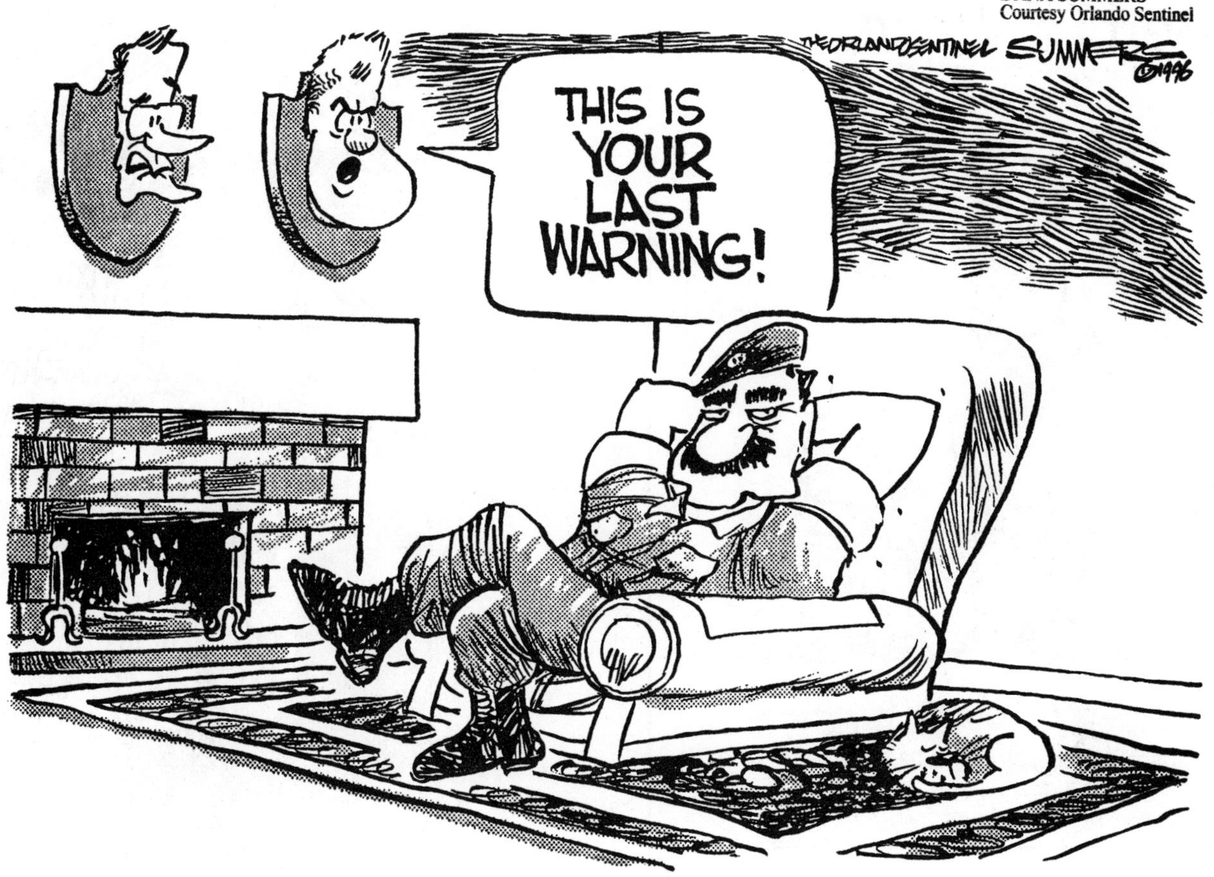
THIS IS YOUR LAST WARNING!

THOMAS BOLDT
Courtesy Calgary Herald

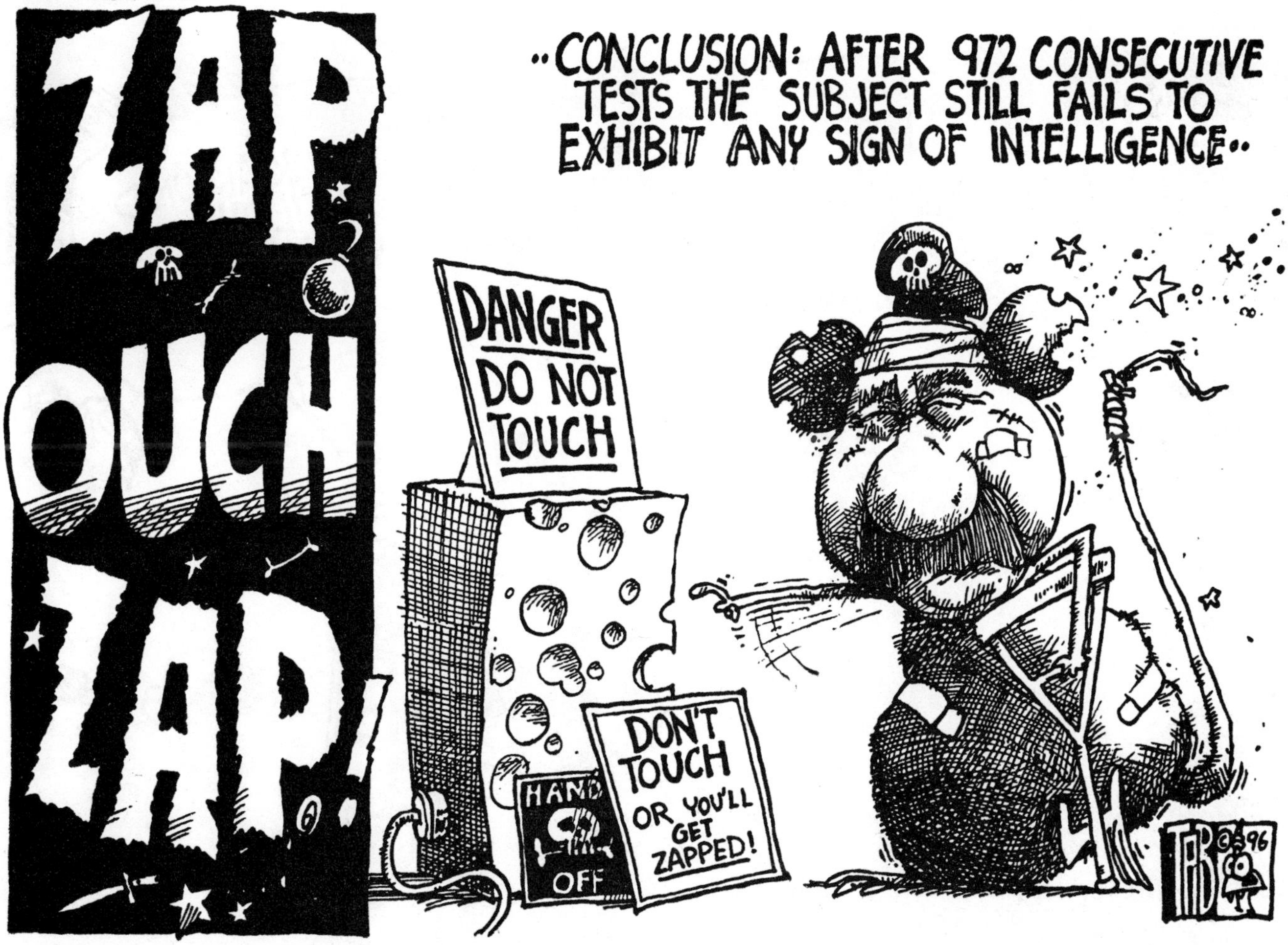
..CONCLUSION: AFTER 972 CONSECUTIVE TESTS THE SUBJECT STILL FAILS TO EXHIBIT ANY SIGN OF INTELLIGENCE..
ZAP OUCH ZAP!
DANGER DO NOT TOUCH
DON'T TOUCH OR YOU'LL GET ZAPPED!
OFF

Berry's World

"Gosh, I hope you won't be offended. We have changed the designation 'Most-Favored' to 'Normal' trade relations."

© 1996 by NEA, Inc.

JIM BERRY
Courtesy NEA

JOHN KNUDSEN
Courtesy St. Louis Review

MIKE KEEFE
Courtesy Denver Post

ALAN KING
Courtesy Ottawa Citizen

JAKE FULLER
Courtesy Gainesville Sun

MALCOLM MAYES
Courtesy Edmonton Journal

THOMAS BOLDT
Courtesy Calgary Herald

96

FRED CURATOLO
Courtesy Edmonton Sun

GUY BADEAUX
Courtesy Le Droit, Ottawa

GUY BADEAUX
Courtesy Le Droit, Ottawa

BRUCE BEATTIE
Courtesy Daytona Beach News-Journal

MARK BREWER
Courtesy The Hour (Conn.)

MARKSTUDIO@AOL.COM

BRIAN GABLE
Courtesy Toronto Globe and Mail

REX BABIN
Courtesy Albany Times Union

WEEKEND AT BORIS'

OLD COMMUNISTS NEVER DIE...

JAMES GRASDAL
Courtesy Edmonton Journal

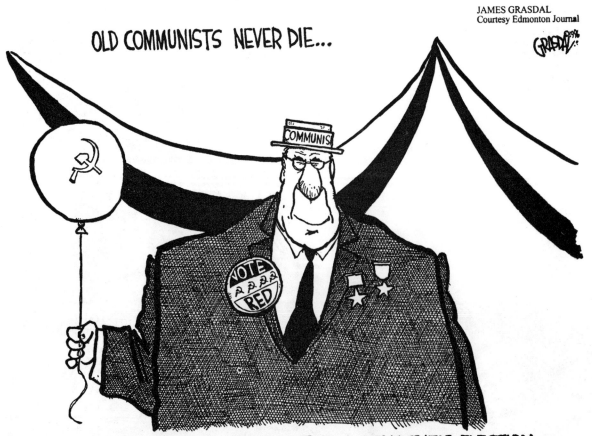

...THEY JUST RUN FOR OFFICE IN A DEMOCRATIC ELECTION...

The Economy

The U.S. economy showed slow, steady growth during 1996, and was picking up steam as the year ended. The deficit was down and unemployment neared a seven-year low. Economic growth for the year was expected to reach 3 percent, and inflation remained under control.

Although the figures were rosy, Americans generally remained lukewarm about the economy. Business downsizing that resulted in thousands of layoffs and the need for two-worker families to make ends meet put a damper on the economic outlook. Workers were feeling insecure. Good-paying jobs were harder to find as many companies moved overseas in search of cheaper labor. The minimum wage increase cost many low-paying jobs that some businesses could no longer afford.

Soaring gas prices brought protests from the driving public during the summer, and small farms continued to shrink as conglomerates grew.

Worldwide, there was a nervous reaction to Federal Reserve Chairman Alan Greenspan's December speech cautioning against "irrational exuberance" in the financial markets. It seemed to demonstrate an uneasiness about the economy which, after a brief pause, resumed its upward climb.

ETTA HULME
Courtesy Ft. Worth Star-Telegram

"AS THE ONLY EMPLOYEE REMAINING ON THE PAYROLL, THERE'S SOMETHING THE BOARD NEEDS TO DISCUSS WITH YOU. IS PRODUCTIVITY GOING TO BE A PROBLEM?"

JIMMY MARGULIES
Courtesy The Record (N.J.)/
North America Syndicate (by permission)

JIM MORIN
Courtesy Miami Herald

JAMES GRASDAL
Courtesy Edmonton Journal

ANN CLEAVES
Courtesy La Prensa (San Diego)

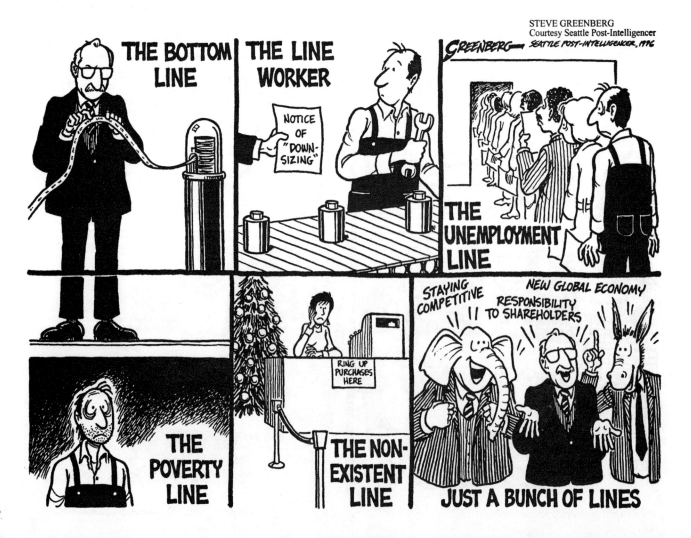

STEVE GREENBERG
Courtesy Seattle Post-Intelligencer

104

DAVE SATTLER
Courtesy Journal and Courier (Ind.)

TED RALL
Courtesy Chronicle Features

THE C.E.O. AT HOME

MIKE KEEFE
Courtesy Denver Post

MIKE LUCKOVICH
Courtesy Atlanta Constitution

JOE HOFFECKER
Courtesy Cincinnati Business Courier

TWISTER II

106

NEIL GRAHAME
Courtesy Spencer Newspapers

TIM BENSON
Courtesy Sioux Falls Argus Leader

GEORGE DANBY
Courtesy Bangor Daily News

JIMMY MARGULIES
Courtesy The Record (N.J.)/
North America Syndicate (by permission)

ED GAMBLE
Courtesy Florida Times-Union

ED FISCHER
Courtesy Rochester Post-Bulletin

BUBBA FLINT
Courtesy Arlington Morning News

SCOTT BATEMAN
Courtesy Eugene Register Guard (Ore.)

DENNY PRITCHARD
Courtesy Ottawa Citizen

JOE HOFFECKER
Courtesy Cincinnati Business Courier

JOHN MARSHALL
Courtesy Binghampton Press and Sun-Bulletin

TED RALL
Courtesy Chronicle Features

JOHN SPENCER
Courtesy Philadelphia Business Journal

Health

Several states filed suits against large tobacco companies, contending that they concealed information about the dangers of tobacco and manipulated nicotine levels to keep smokers hooked. The lawsuits sought to force tobacco companies to pay some of the medical costs connected to smoking.

President Clinton recognized the issue as a popular one with the voters and seized it during the campaign. All the while the Clinton Administration had no strong policy against drugs—in fact, many White House staffers acknowledged having been drug users.

Although charges by veterans of the Gulf War that they had been exposed to chemical and biological weapons were first rejected by the Department of Defense, the Pentagon later admitted that Iraqi chemical weapons sites had been bombed and poison gas could have been released.

News broke during the year that many Americans—including high-income physicians—had defaulted on their government college loans. Congressmen demanded that they be made to pay up, but President Clinton insisted that the rate of default was declining because of tougher screening and stronger collection efforts.

Dr. Jack Kevorkian remained in the news by helping more of the terminally ill commit suicide.

JERRY BARNETT
Courtesy Indianapolis News

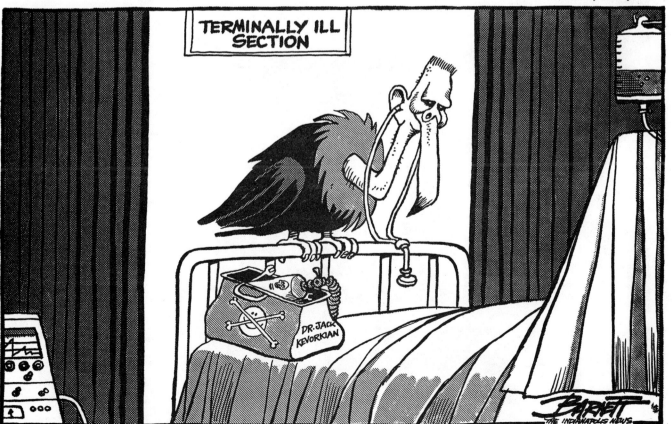

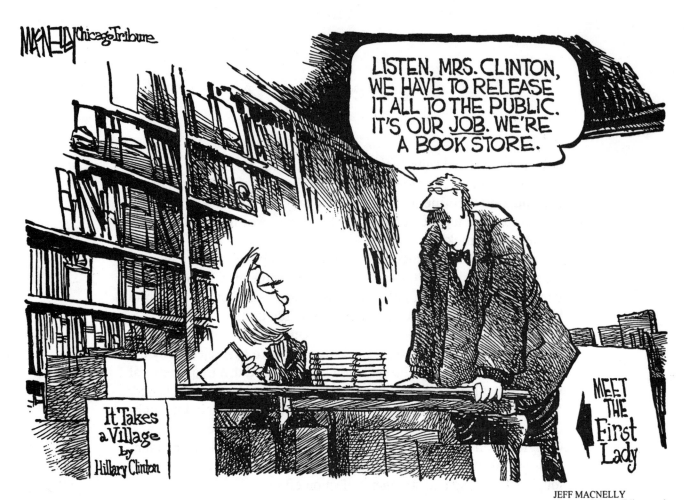

JEFF MACNELLY
Courtesy Chicago Tribune and
Tribune Media Services

MICHAEL RAMIREZ
Courtesy Memphis Commercial Appeal

EDDIE GERMANO
Courtesy The Enterprise (Mass.)

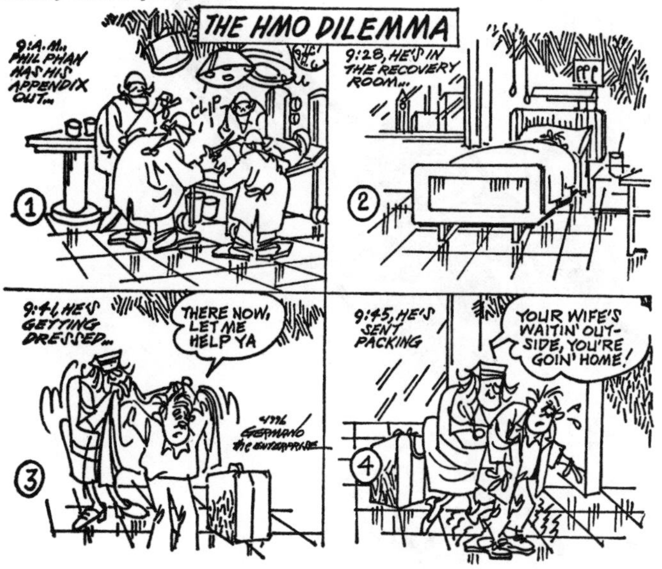
THE HMO DILEMMA
9 A.M., PHIL PHAN HAS HIS APPENDIX OUT...
CLIP
9:28, HE'S IN THE RECOVERY ROOM...
9:41, HE'S GETTING DRESSED...
THERE NOW, LET ME HELP YA
9:45, HE'S SENT PACKING
YOUR WIFE'S WAITIN' OUT-SIDE, YOU'RE GOIN' HOME!

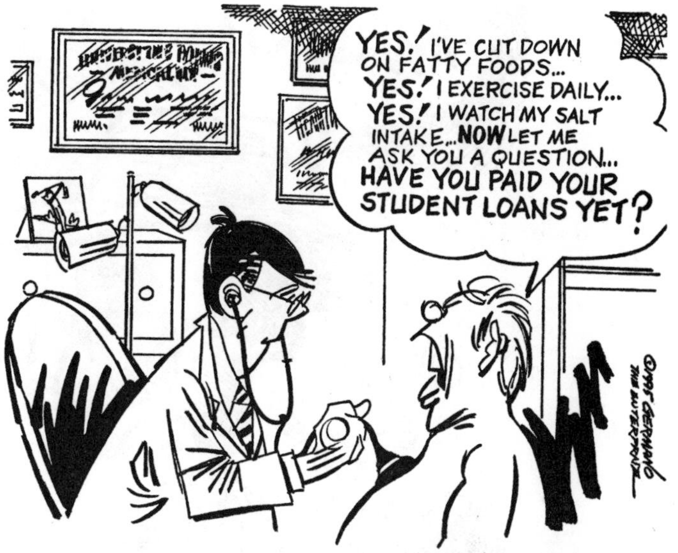
YES! I'VE CUT DOWN ON FATTY FOODS... YES! I EXERCISE DAILY... YES! I WATCH MY SALT INTAKE... NOW LET ME ASK YOU A QUESTION... HAVE YOU PAID YOUR STUDENT LOANS YET?

EDDIE GERMANO
Courtesy The Enterprise (Mass.)

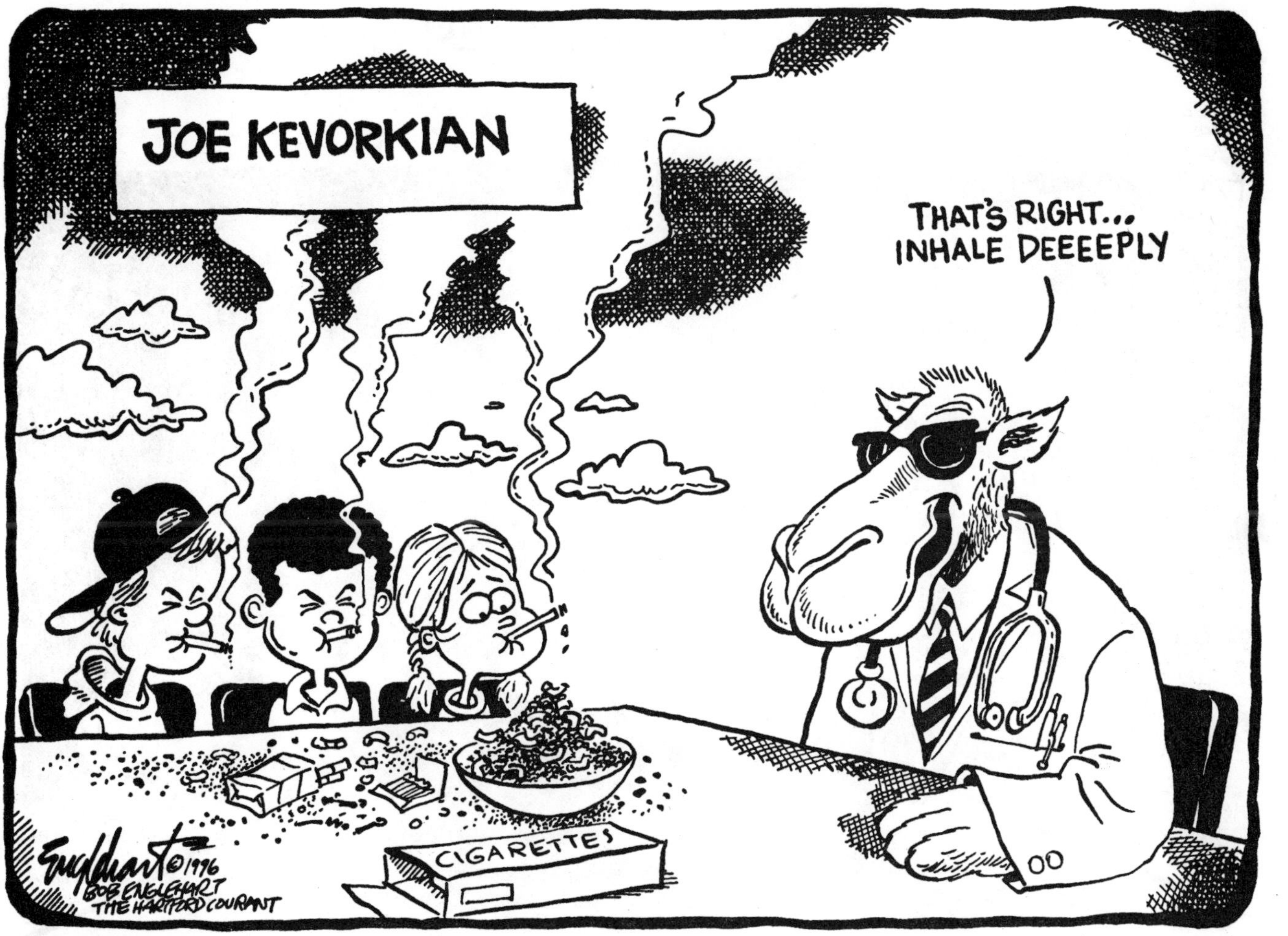
JOE KEVORKIAN
THAT'S RIGHT... INHALE DEEEEPLY
CIGARETTES
Englehart ©1996 BOB ENGLEHART THE HARTFORD COURANT

BOB ENGLEHART
Courtesy Hartford Courant

LOU GRANT
Courtesy The Montclarion (Calif.)

STEVE BREEN
Courtesy Asbury Park Press (N.J.)

JEFF LITTLE
Courtesy Erie Morning News

MICHAEL GILLETT
Courtesy Lancaster Eagle-Gazette (Ohio)

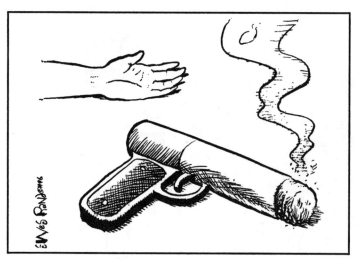

WES RAND
Courtesy Norwich Bulletin

LARRY WRIGHT
Courtesy Detroit News

JOE LONG
Courtesy Little Falls Evening Times (N.Y.)

KEVIN KALLAUGH
Courtesy Baltimore Sun

BOB DORNFRIED
Courtesy Fairfield Citizen

PAYNE

EUGENE PAYNE
Courtesy Charlotte Observer

DANA SUMMERS
Courtesy Orlando Sentinel

GARY BROOKINS
Courtesy Richmond Times-Dispatch

WAYNE STROOT
Courtesy Hastings Tribune

BOB DORNFRIED
Courtesy Greenwich News

CHARLES DANIEL
Courtesy Knoxville News-Sentinel

JEFF MACNELLY
Courtesy Chicago Tribune and
Tribune Media Services

The Family

When in 1992 Vice-president Dan Quayle said in a speech that traditional family values were deteriorating and that morality must be restored to American society, he was ridiculed by liberals across the land. Democrats, comedians, and the media had a field day depicting him as a dolt and a clown. Many of them have now had second thoughts. President Clinton strongly endorsed the Quayle position in his re-election campaign, using the issue as though it was his idea from the beginning.

Drug use among teens declined for a time, but in 1996 began rising again. A government survey released in September showed that drug use among the 12-to-17 age group had more than doubled since 1992. More sports figures were found to be using drugs, and members of the White House staff admitted to drug use.

Same-sex marriages became an issue in 1996 as Hawaii moved toward recognizing such unions. Congress passed a law making such marriages illegal.

The outlook for saving Social Security was not promising at year's end. A special panel studying ways to keep the program solvent failed after two years to come up with a solution.

GARY VARVEL
Courtesy Indianapolis Star

PATRICK RICE
Courtesy Jupiter Courier

CHUCK ASAY
Courtesy Colorado Springs Gazette Telegraph

124

CURTIS

CHRIS CURTIS
Courtesy The Connection (Va.)

GARY VARVEL
Courtesy Indianapolis Star

Gary Varvel
THE INDIANAPOLIS STAR

"Forgive me, Lord.   I . . . I . . . I watched 'Bambi.' "

ETTA HULME
Courtesy Ft. Worth Star-Telegram
©1996 FORT WORTH STAR-TELEGRAM

KEVIN KALLAUGHER
Courtesy Baltimore Sun

ED GAMBLE
Courtesy Florida Times-Union

DAVE SATTLER
Courtesy Journal and Courier (Ind.)

BRIAN DUFFY
Courtesy Des Moines Register

ALAN VITELLO
Courtesy Daily Reporter-Herald (Colo.)

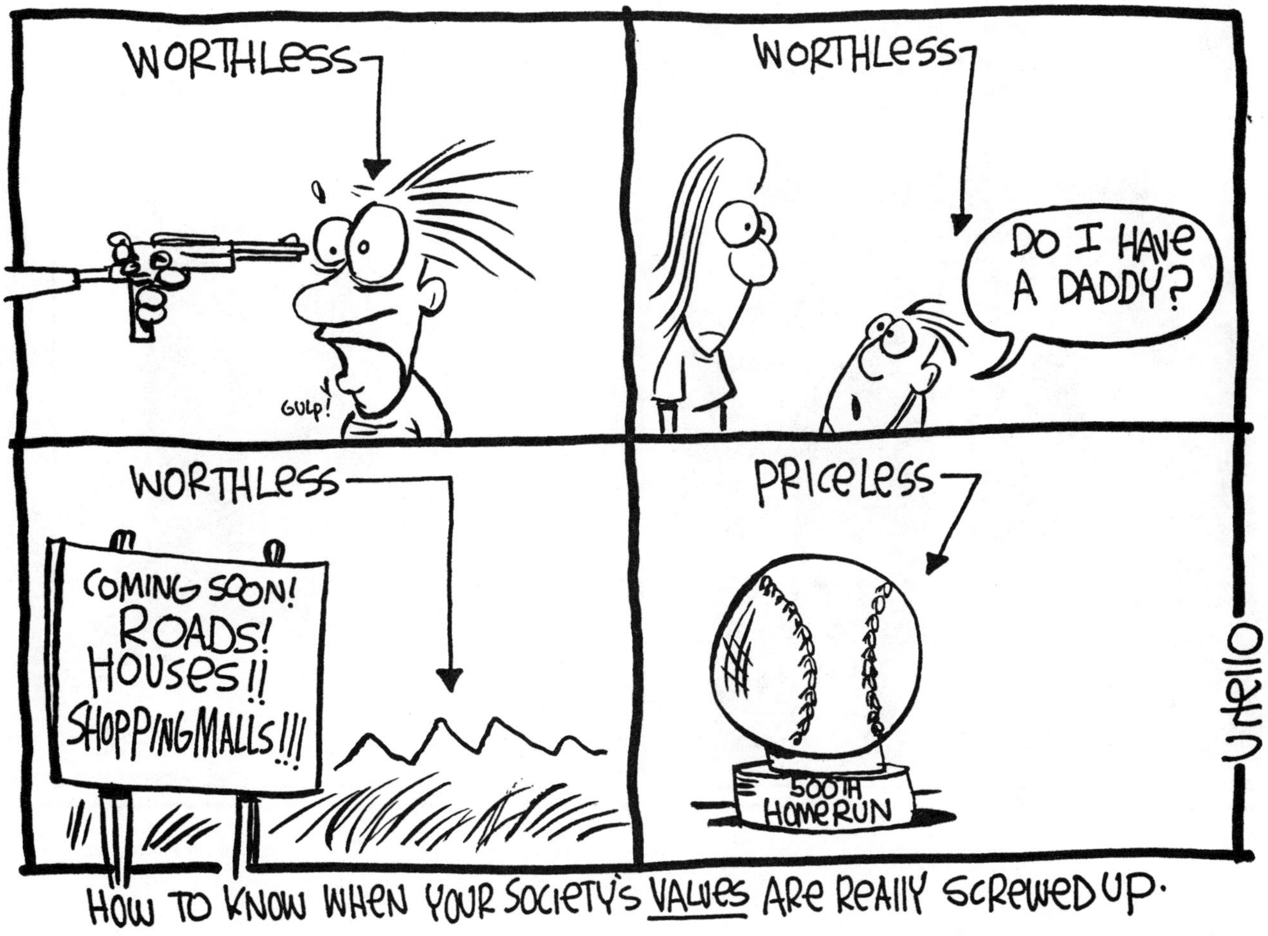
WORTHLESS
GULP!
WORTHLESS
DO I HAVE A DADDY?
WORTHLESS
COMING SOON! ROADS! HOUSES!! SHOPPING MALLS!!!
PRICELESS
500TH HOME RUN
VITELLO
HOW TO KNOW WHEN YOUR SOCIETY'S VALUES ARE REALLY SCREWED UP.

GARY VARVEL
Courtesy Indianapolis Star

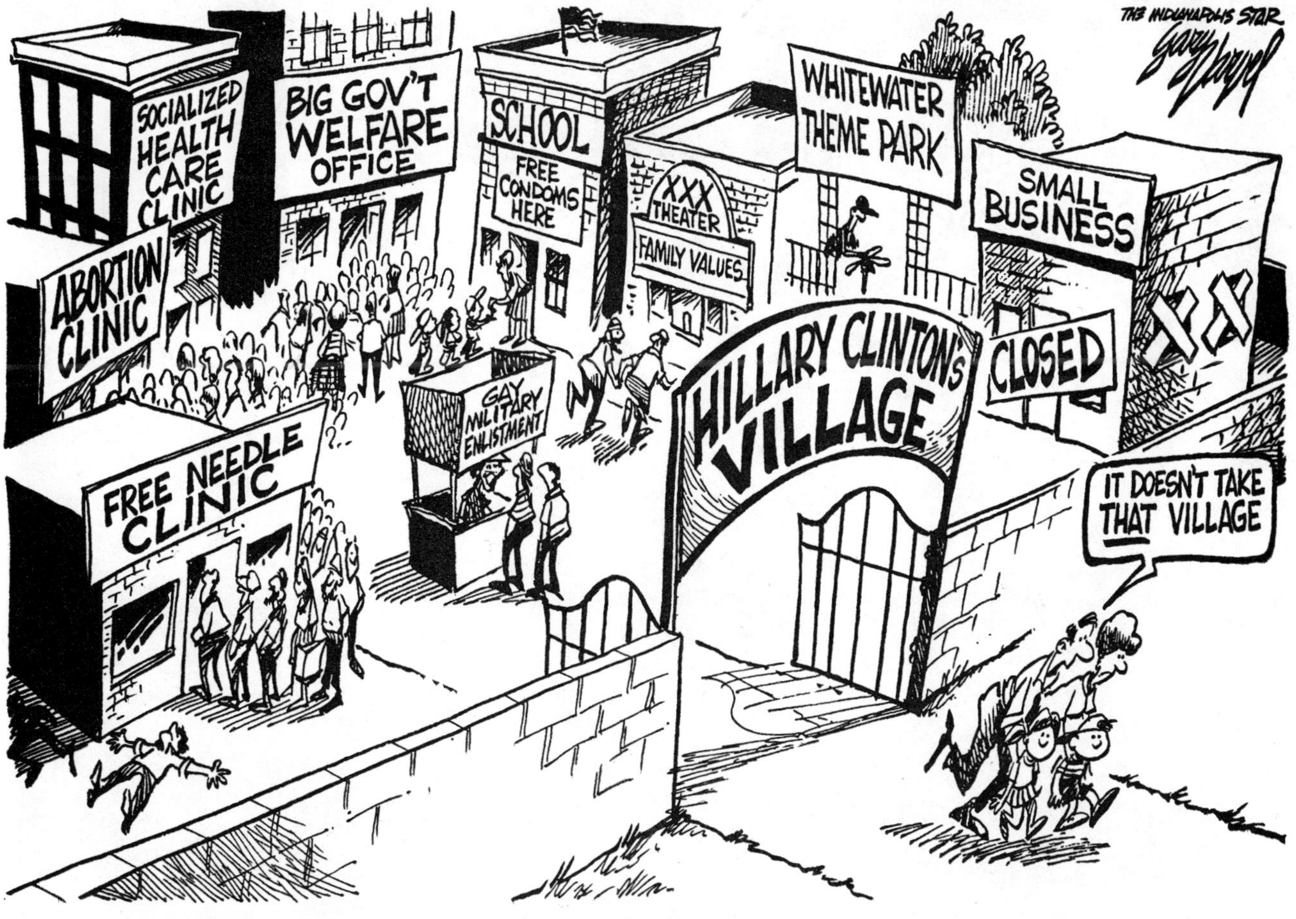
THE INDIANAPOLIS STAR
GARY VARVEL
SOCIALIZED HEALTH CARE CLINIC
BIG GOV'T WELFARE OFFICE
SCHOOL
FREE CONDOMS HERE
XXX THEATER
FAMILY VALUES
WHITEWATER THEME PARK
SMALL BUSINESS
ABORTION CLINIC
GAY MILITARY ENLISTMENT
HILLARY CLINTON'S VILLAGE
CLOSED
FREE NEEDLE CLINIC
IT DOESN'T TAKE THAT VILLAGE

SCOTT STANTIS
Courtesy Birmingham News

MICHAEL RAMIREZ
Courtesy Memphis Commercial Appeal

130

Welfare and the Poor

President Clinton vowed to "end welfare as we know it" and late in the year, even though he viewed the new welfare bill as "seriously flawed," signed it into law. Basically, the new legislation discontinues Aid to Families with Dependent Children. This 60-year-old program had guaranteed the nation's needy a federal safety net. The needy must now look to the states for help. Recipients will be required to work, and there is a lifetime limit of five years of federal aid. Cuts also are being made in the food stamp program and in aid to disabled children and immigrants.

The new program is intended to encourage people to do for themselves—and for the government to help them do it. Many groups claim the new approach won't work, that the states do not have the money to take on this task. Social workers predict that the new law will push more families into poverty.

Under the new reform law, most immigrants will be ineligible for most government social programs. Any individual who manages to participate in a forbidden program for twelve months will face deportation.

CLYDE WELLS
Courtesy Augusta Chronicle

1996, SEATTLE POST-INTELLIGENCER GREENBERG

STEVE GREENBERG
Courtesy Seattle Post-Intelligencer

GARY MARKSTEIN
Courtesy Milwaukee Journal Sentinel

IT TAKES A VILLAGE TO ABANDON A CHILD

MIKE LUCKOVICH
Courtesy Atlanta Constitution

MATT WUERKER
Courtesy Los Angeles Times

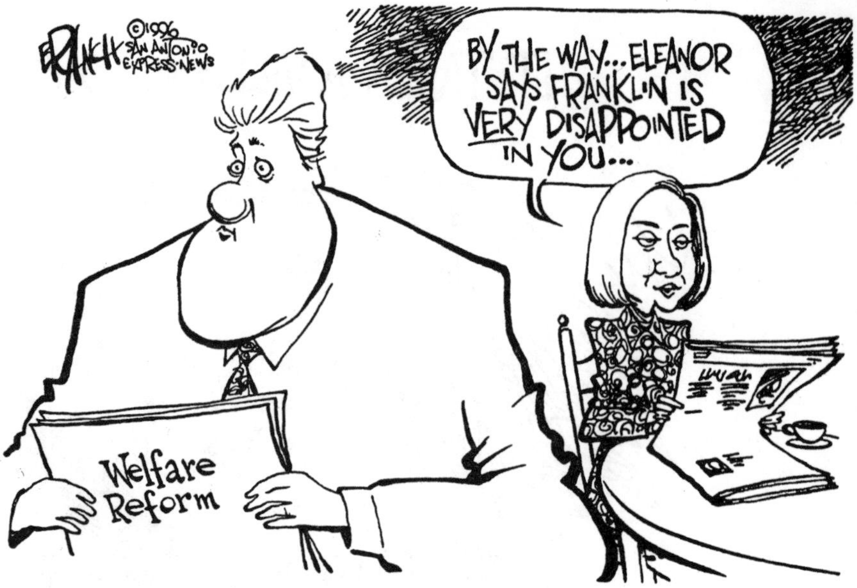
BY THE WAY... ELEANOR SAYS FRANKLIN IS VERY DISAPPOINTED IN YOU...
Welfare Reform

JOHN BRANCH
Courtesy San Antonio Express-News

DENNIS DRAUGHON
Courtesy Scranton Times

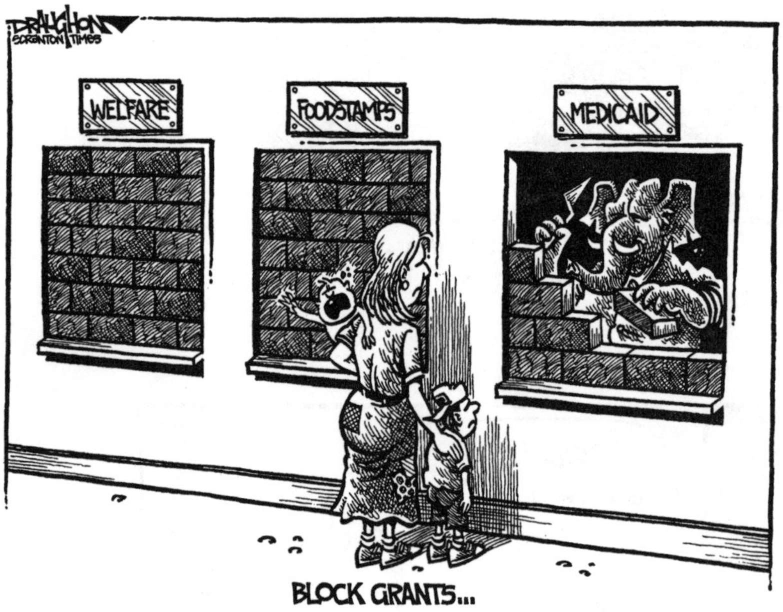
WELFARE
FOODSTAMPS
MEDICAID
BLOCK GRANTS...

STEVE LINDSTROM
Courtesy Duluth News-Tribune

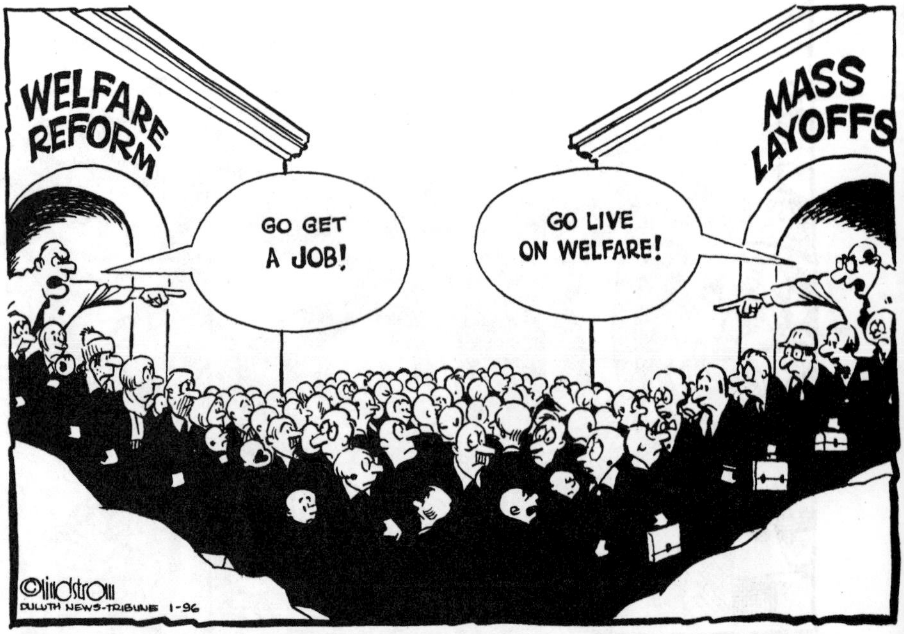
WELFARE REFORM
MASS LAYOFFS
GO GET A JOB!
GO LIVE ON WELFARE!

RANDY WICKS
Courtesy Valencia Signal (Calif.)

STEVE KELLEY
Courtesy San Diego Union

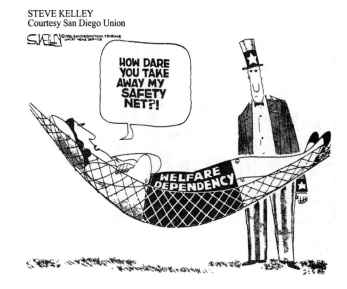

ANNETTE BALESTERI
Courtesy Antioch Daily Ledger (Calif.)

CLAY BENNETT
Courtesy North America Syndicate

PAUL CONRAD
Courtesy L.A. Times Syndicate

SCOTT WILLIS
Courtesy San Jose Mercury

The Military

News broke late in the year that female Army recruits were being abused and sexually harassed. The Army quickly brought court-martial charges against two drill instructors and a company commander at the Aberdeen Ordnance Center, alleging sexual misconduct with female solders. Officials expressed particular concern about the prospect of trainers taking advantage of their charges.

It was learned during the year that the U.S. provides highly sophisticated weapons and military equipment to just about anyone with the money to buy—including foreign enemies. And it is not only U.S. businesses doing the selling. Now the Pentagon has gotten in on the action. With the downsizing of the military, the vast agency's surplus sales system has become overloaded. Foreign buyers are purchasing much of this surplus and shipping it overseas to countries such as Iraq, Iran, Libya, China, and Cuba.

The Supreme Court finally ruled that the Virginia Military Institute's all-male admissions policy violated women's constitutional rights to equal protection.

JEFF KOTERBA
Courtesy Omaha World-Herald

137

KIRK ANDERSON
Courtesy St. Paul Pioneer Press

"THE ARMY IS COMMITTED TO FINDING PLACES FOR WOMEN TO SERVE."

JERRY HOLBERT
Courtesy Boston Herald

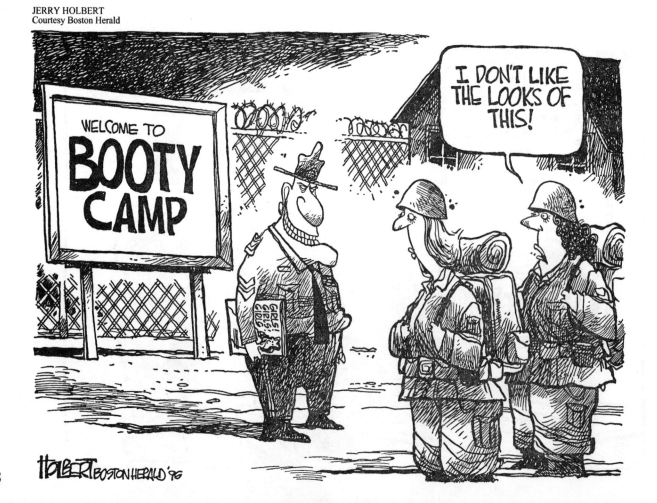

DENNIS DRAUGHON
Courtesy Scranton Times

DRAUGHON SCRANTON TIMES
CANDID DISCUSSION OF GULF WAR SYNDROME
ENTER HERE

BATTLE CRIES
STANTIS ©1996 THE BIRMINGHAM NEWS
MAKE THE WORLD SAFE FOR DEMOCRACY !!!
REMEMBER PEARL HARBOR!!!
WHY THE HECK AM I HERE?
SOMALIA
BOSNIA
HAITI
ZAIRE

SCOTT STANTIS
Courtesy Birmingham News

JACK MCLEOD
Courtesy Federal Times

JEFF STAHLER
Courtesy Cincinnati Post

CHARLES DANIEL
Courtesy Knoxville News-Sentinel

GILL FOX
Courtesy Connecticut Post

CHUCK ASAY
Courtesy Colorado Springs Gazette Telegraph

DOUGLAS REGALIA
Courtesy San Ramon Valley Times (Calif.)

PAUL SZEP
Courtesy Boston Globe

STUDENT TEST SCORES INDICATE 7 YEAR BILLIONS OF DOLLARS REFORM OF PUBLIC SCHOOLS A COSTLY FAILURE

MARK THORNHILL
Courtesy North County Times (Calif.)

Education

The cost of a college education in the United States continued to outpace inflation. College costs during the year rose 6 percent at public four-year colleges while inflation increased only 2.4 percent. New data released shows that in rankings of eighth-grade achievement among the nations of the world, U.S. students placed seventeenth in science and twenty-eighth in mathematics.

The dropout rate of American students remained much too high, and school facilities across the country continue to deteriorate. Some 59,000 of the nation's school buildings need immediate and extensive repairs at a cost of billions.

A six-year-old student in North Carolina became the youngest person yet to be accused of sexual harassment. The bespectacled first grader was seen kissing a girl on the cheek and was suspended from school. The action brought a flood of criticism, and school officials soon backed down, explaining that they were only following policy prohibiting "unwarranted and unwelcome touching of one student by another."

GARY BROOKINS
Courtesy Richmond Times-Dispatch

143

JAMES MERCADO
Courtesy The Garden Island

JEFF STAHLER
Courtesy Cincinnati Post

MIKE KEEFE
Courtesy Denver Post

JAMES CASCIARI
Courtesy Vero Beach Press Journal

JEFF MACNELLY
Courtesy Chicago Tribune and
Tribune Media Services

WALT HANDELSMAN
Courtesy Times-Picayune (N.O.)

ROB ROGERS
Courtesy Pittsburgh Post-Gazette

PAUL FELL
Courtesy Lincoln Journal

CHRIS OBRION
Courtesy Free Lance-Star (Va.)

CHANGING OF THE GUARD

ED COLLEY
Courtesy Carver Reporter

JACK JURDEN
Courtesy Wilmington News Journal

PATRICK RICE
Courtesy Jupiter Courier

WES RAND
Courtesy Norwich Bulletin

JOHN BRANCH
Courtesy San Antonio Express-News

LARRY WRIGHT
Courtesy Detroit News

BRUCE QUAST
Courtesy Rockford Register-Star

DANA SUMMERS
Courtesy Orlando Sentinel

JEFF MACNELLY
Courtesy Chicago Tribune and
Tribune Media Services

Crime

Former Berkeley professor Ted John Kaczynski, who police say could be the notorious Unabomber, was arrested and accused of possessing materials for making a bomb. The Unabomber, who has killed 3 and injured 23 with bombs since 1978, has issued manifestoes demanding a return to a more primitive standard of living.

After a bomb exploded at Olympic Park in Atlanta during the 1996 Olympic Games, suspicion quickly settled on Richard Jewell, a security guard. After several months of intense investigation, however, the F.B.I. sent Jewell a letter stating that he was not a suspect.

A rash of fires at black churches in the South received national attention, but investigation indicated that few of the burnings were racially motivated. The civil suit against O. J. Simpson got under way late in the year.

Bernard Goetz, who shot four black youths on a New York subway eleven years ago, was ordered to pay damages totaling $43 million. Former Rep. Dan Rostenkowski pleaded guilty to mail fraud and was sentenced to seventeen months in prison.

Serious crime continued to decline for the fourth straight year, dropping 2 percent from 1995.

JIM BORGMAN
Courtesy Cincinnati Enquirer

"OH. AND MR. JEWELL...... HAVE A NICE DAY."

RANDY BISH
Courtesy Tribune-Review (Pa.)

GLENN MCCOY
Courtesy Belleville News-Democrat (Ill.)

MIKE LUCKOVICH
Courtesy Atlanta Constitution

RICHARD JEWEL

FBI

JANET RENO

©1996 Chicago Tribune

DICK LOCHER
Courtesy Chicago Tribune

MIKE PETERS
Courtesy Dayton Daily News
http://www.grimmy.com
©1996 Dayton Daily News
Tribune Media Service

the FBI OLYMPICS

100 METER RUSH TO JUDGEMENT

SYNCHRONIZED INDICTMENTS

THE LEAK AND RUMOR RELAY

THE BROAD JUMP TO CONCLUSION

"...AND YOU HAVE TO WONDER WHAT COULD DRIVE SOMEONE TO SUCH A PROFOUND LOATHING OF OUR MODERN TECHNOLOGICAL SOCIETY..."

VIC HARVILLE
Courtesy Arkansas Democrat-Gazette

JOHN TREVER
Courtesy Albuquerque Journal

DOUG MACGREGOR
Courtesy Ft. Meyers News-Press

PAUL SZEP
Courtesy Boston Globe

BOB GORRELL
Courtesy Richmond Times-Dispatch

"GIVE US A WHILE . . . . WE CAN PIN THIS ON HIM!"

RALPH DUNAGIN
Courtey Orlando Sentinel

RALPH DUNAGIN
Courtey Orlando Sentinel

"YOUR HONOR, MR. KACYNSKI WOULD LIKE TO ENTER AS EVIDENCE..."

NEWS ITEM:
BABY-BOOMER PARENTS **EXPECT** THEIR KIDS TO TRY ILLEGAL DRUGS.

(SNIFF)
HEH, HEH, LOOK MOON-BEAM, OUR LITTLE BOY HAS DROPPED HIS **FIRST ACID** ...

GROOVY!

BOB LANG
Courtesy News-Sentinel (Ind.)

ROBERT ARIAIL
Courtesy The State (S.C.)

"... HONEST, I'M WITH THE OLYMPICS — I DON'T KNOW <u>ANYTHING</u> ABOUT THOSE CHURCH FIRES!"

JON RICHARDS
Courtesy Santa Fe Reporter

JOHN DEROSIER
Courtesy Mobile Press Register

ETTA HULME
Courtesy Ft. Worth Star-Telegram

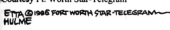

OSWALDO SAGASTEGUI
Courtesy Excelsior (Mex.)

JEFF KOTERBA
Courtesy Omaha World-Herald

ALAN KING
Courtesy Ottawa Citizen

ED GAMBLE
Courtesy Florida Times-Union

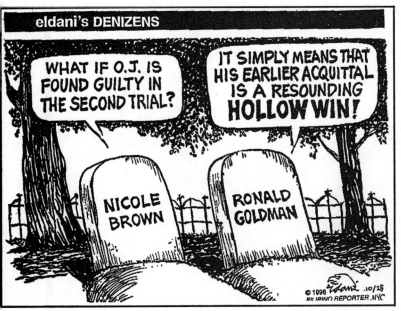

eldani's DENIZENS

WHAT IF O.J. IS FOUND GUILTY IN THE SECOND TRIAL?

IT SIMPLY MEANS THAT HIS EARLIER ACQUITTAL IS A RESOUNDING HOLLOW WIN!

NICOLE BROWN

RONALD GOLDMAN

© 1996 FILIPINO REPORTER, NYC .10/25

DANI AGUILA
Courtesy Filipino Reporter

News item: O.J. hosts domestic violence fund-raiser...

YARD SALE

BEST OFFER

DAVID GRANLUND
Courtesy Middlesex News

EUGENE PAYNE
Courtesy Charlotte Observer

YOU'RE FREE TO GO NOW. MR. JEWELL!

FBI

ROY PETERSON
Courtesy Vancouver Sun

ROY PETERSON
Courtesy Vancouver Sun

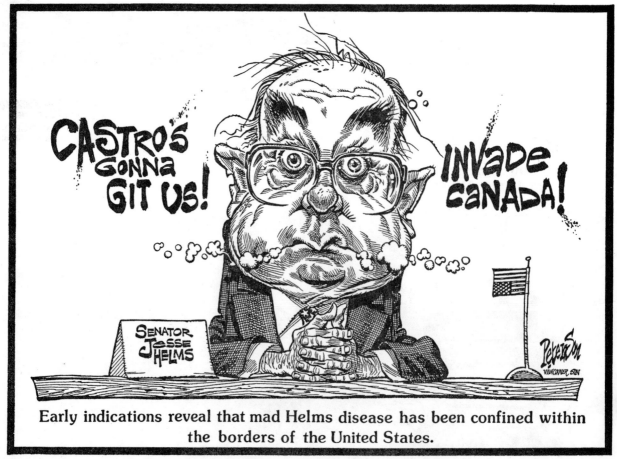

Early indications reveal that mad Helms disease has been confined within the borders of the United States.

Canada

The Helms-Burton Act, which makes foreign companies that profit from American property expropriated in Cuba liable in American courts, was signed into law in March. Canada has always enjoyed reasonable relations with Cuba, and the new law put a crimp in trade with the island nation. Helms-Burton was intended to punish Cuba, but has made America's allies who trade with that country unhappy.

Canada's long-established medicare system has not escaped funding cutbacks, and many doctors are moving to the U.S. Canadian industry continued to downsize, bringing bad news to many workers.

As the vote by Quebec on whether to separate from Canada approached in late 1995, much of the nation went into a frenzied flag-waving act, trying to persuade the unhappy province not to withdraw. As a result, the maple-leaf flag was seen everywhere. This patriotic outpouring continued throughout 1996 in an effort to convince Quebec not to vote to separate in the future.

MALCOLM MAYES
Courtesy Edmonton Journal

INTERFERENCE DAY.

STEPHEN NEASE
Courtesy Montreal Gazette

DAN MURPHY
Courtesy Vancouver Province

FRED CURATOLO
Courtesy Edmonton Sun

ANDY DONATO
Courtesy Toronto Sun

BILL HOGAN
Courtesy Times-Transcript (N. Bruns.)

Realizing he could incur the wrath of the
Chief Electoral Officer of Quebec and quite
possibly influence the outcome of the next
referendum, Winslow threw caution
to the wind and bought the little
flag anyway.

MERLE R. TINGLEY
Courtesy Montreal Gazette

DENNY PRITCHARD
Courtesy Ottawa Citizen

MERLE R. TINGLEY
Courtesy Montreal Gazette

166

STEPHEN NEASE
Courtesy Toronto Star

ROY PETERSON
Courtesy Vancouver Sun

..ME BRUDDER'S BOY!

BILL HOGAN
Courtesy Times-Transcript (N. Bruns.)

MALCOLM MAYES
Courtesy Edmonton Journal

EVIDENCE SUGGESTS THE EXISTENCE OF PRIMITIVE LIFE FORMS, NOW EXTINCT.

DITTO...

Air Travel

Moments after taking off from Kennedy International Airport on July 17, 1996, T.W.A. Flight 800 exploded over the Atlantic, killing all 230 people aboard. Charred bodies and debris were collected for months, but at year's end investigators still had not been able to explain the tragedy.

On May 11, ValuJet 592 plunged into the Florida Everglades, killing all 110 passengers and crew. Recovery was difficult since divers had to wear special protective suits as they searched in swamps infested with snakes and alligators. The crash was blamed on improperly boxed oxygen canisters, and the small, super-cheap airline was grounded for fifteen weeks because of inadequate inspection and maintenance.

It was revealed that Federal Aviation Administration officials had concerns for months before the crash about possible problems at Valu-Jet. Under pressure from Congress, the F.A.A. began to review its policies for overseeing aviation safety.

ED GAMBLE
Courtesy Florida Times-Union

NICK ANDERSON
Courtesy Louisville Courier Journal

MIKE SMITH
Courtesy Las Vegas Sun

JEFF STAHLER
Courtesy Cincinnati Post

TOM ENGELHARDT
Courtesy St. Louis Post-Dispatch

A Hole In The Sky . . . And In Our Hearts

DON LANDGREN, JR.
Courtesy Clinton Daily Item (Mass.)

ARRIVALS

DEPARTURES

YOUR AIRLINE'S MAINTENANCE RECORD

©1996 FORT MYERS NEWS-PRESS

DOUG MACGREGOR
Courtesy Ft. Meyers News-Press

FBI

FLIGHT 800

MIKE SMITH
Courtesy Las Vegas Sun

172

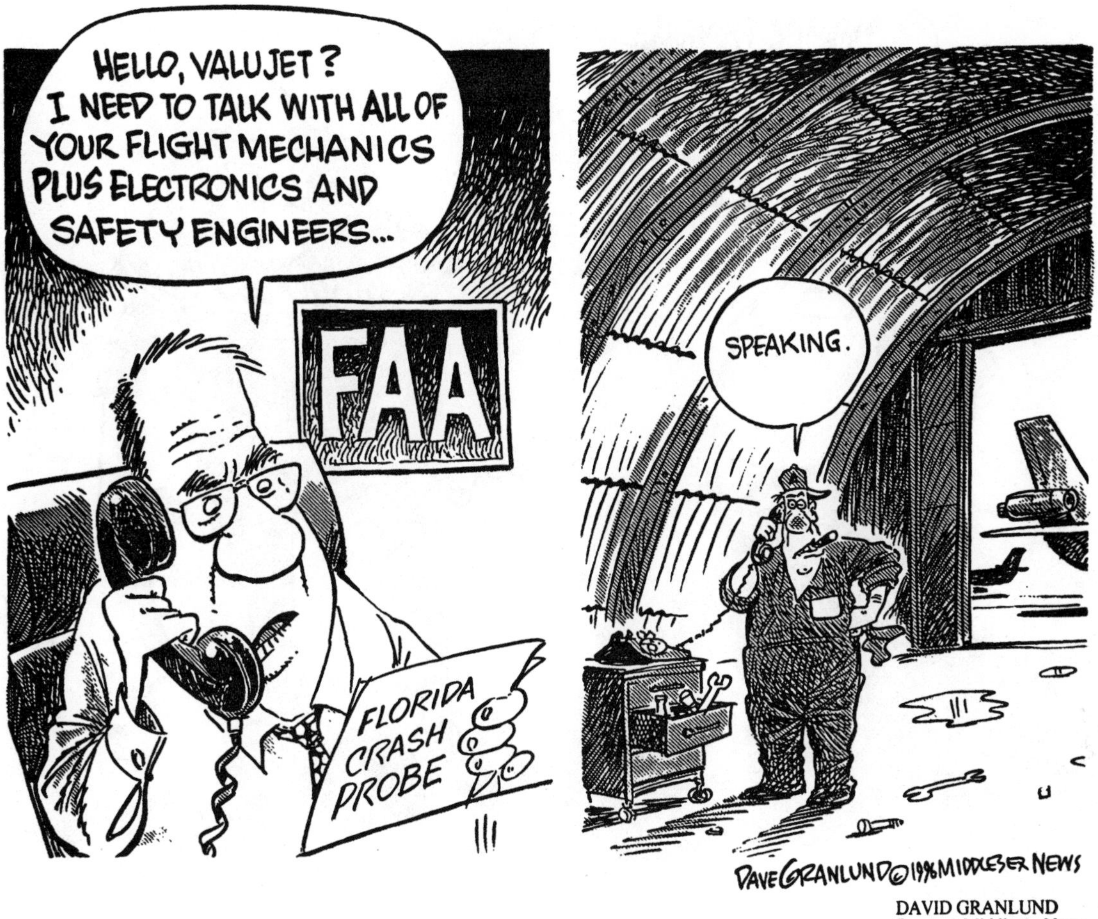
HELLO, VALUJET? I NEED TO TALK WITH ALL OF YOUR FLIGHT MECHANICS PLUS ELECTRONICS AND SAFETY ENGINEERS...
FAA
FLORIDA CRASH PROBE
SPEAKING.
DAVE GRANLUND © 1996 MIDDLESEX NEWS

DAVID GRANLUND
Courtesy Middlesex News

JACK HIGGINS
Courtesy Chicago Sun-Times

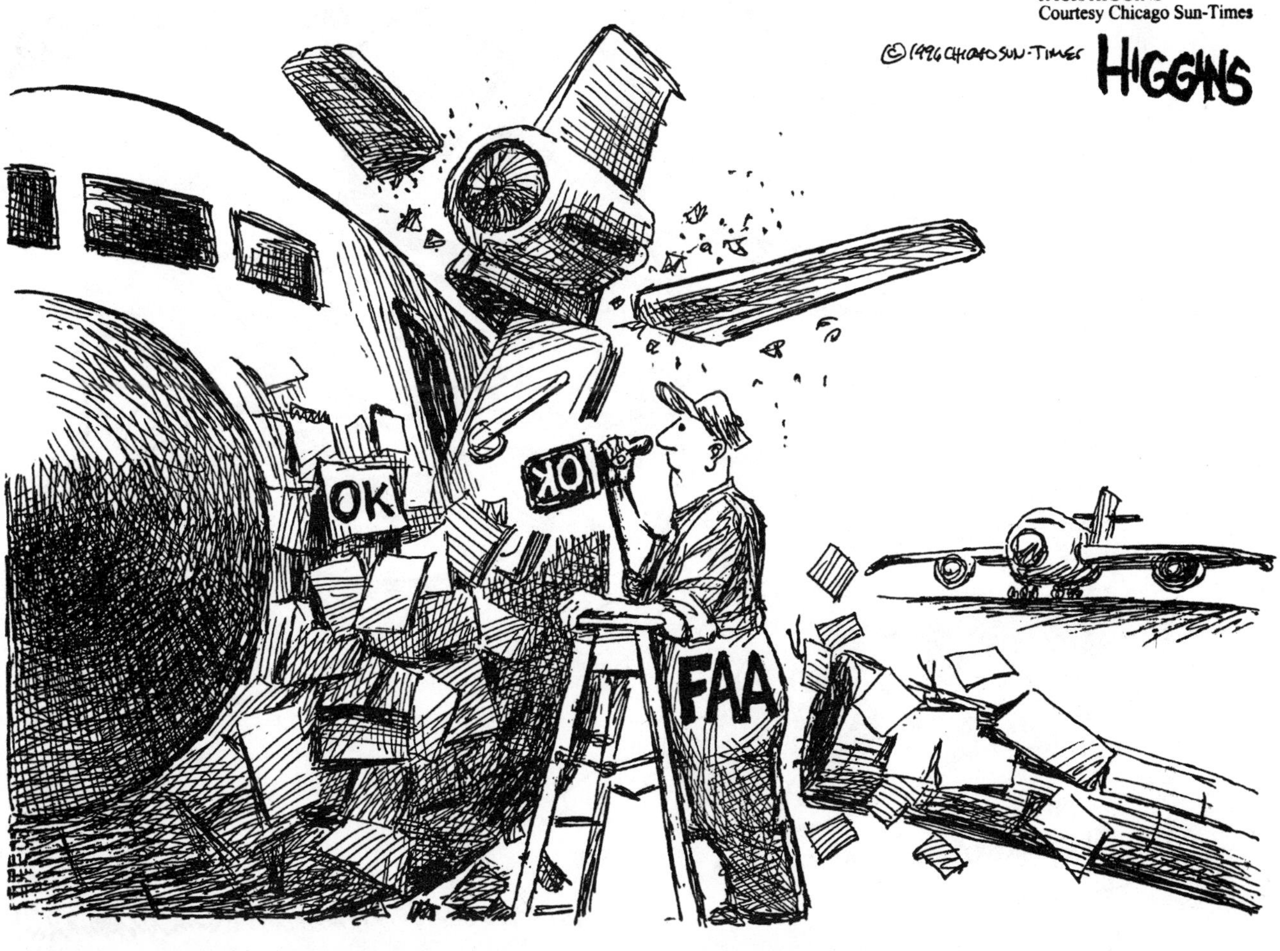
© 1996 CHICAGO SUN-TIMES HIGGINS
OK
OK
FAA

CLYDE WELLS
Courtesy Augusta Chronicle

JAMES LARRICK
Courtesy Columbus Dispatch

Sports

The Olympic Games opened in July in Atlanta amid a sea of hype and hoopla. The city had gone all-out to insure the safety of the athletes and visitors, but the dreaded happened. A bomb exploded at Olympic Park, killing 2 and injuring more than 100. The investigation focused on a security guard, Richard Jewell, but months later the F.B.I. acknowledged he was no longer a suspect.

A highlight of the Games was the heart of little Kerri Strug, who performed despite an ankle injury and helped the U.S. women gymnasts win their first gold medal. Commercialization was worse than ever, with symbols, slogans, and advertisements all over the place.

Shaquille O'Neal, the 7-foot-1-inch basketball star of the Orlando Magics, signed a 7-year contract with the Los Angeles Lakers for $121 million, the richest agreement ever for a professional athlete. Marge Schott, owner of the Cincinnati Reds, was forced to give up day-to-day control of the team because of remarks about Adolf Hitler. Robbie Alomar of the San Diego Padres allegedly spit on an umpire during a game, and disciplinary action was taken by the league.

Owners of sports franchises continued to threaten to move their teams to other cities if new stadiums were not built. Owner Art Modell shifted his National Football League team from Cleveland to Baltimore.

DAVID GRANLUND
Courtesy Middlesex News

The spirit of the games

FRED SEBASTIAN
Courtesy Ottawa Citizen

MICHAEL CAVNA
Courtesy San Diego Union-Tribune

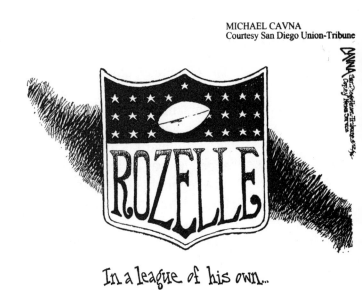

ROZELLE

In a league of his own...

LARRY'S PENCILS 5¢ Official Sponsor 1996 SUMMER GAMES

DREW SHENEMAN
Courtesy Detroit News

RICK KOLLINGER
Courtesy Easton Star Democrat (Md.)

JACK HIGGINS
Courtesy Chicago Sun-Times

MICHAEL CAVNA
Courtesy San Diego Union-Tribune

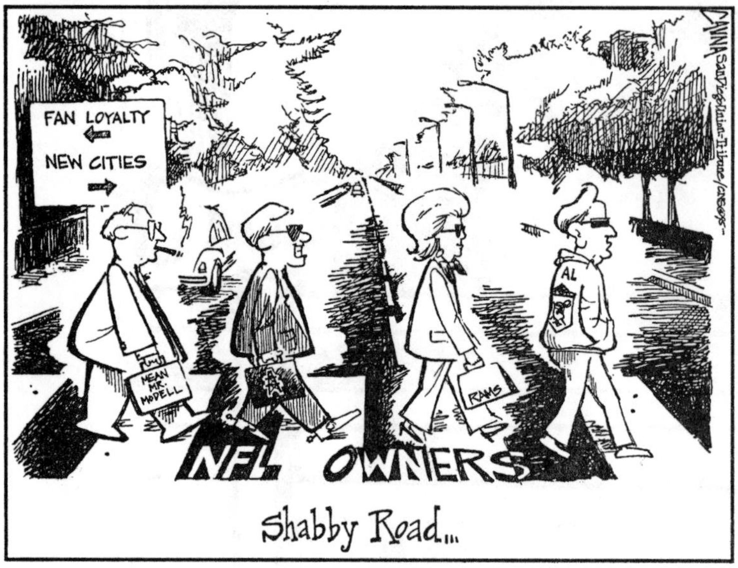
FAN LOYALTY
NEW CITIES
MEAN MR. MODELL
RAMS
AL
NFL OWNERS
Shabby Road...

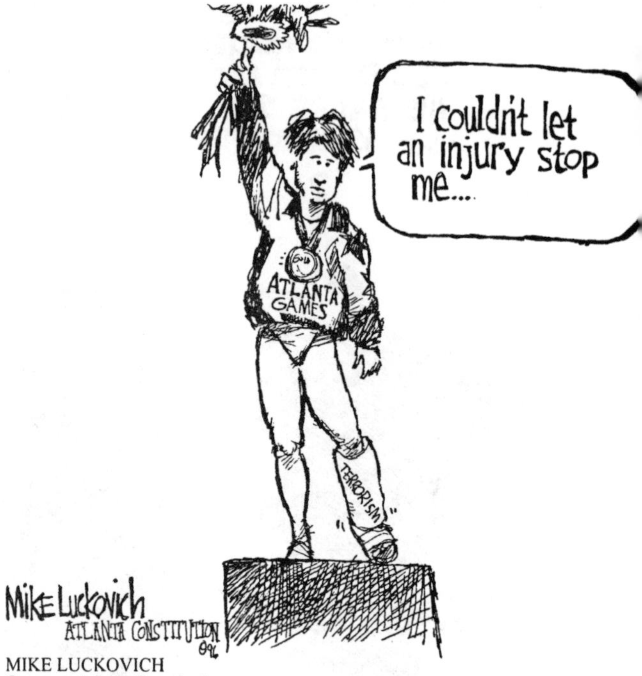
I couldn't let an injury stop me....
ATLANTA GAMES
TERRORISM
Mike Luckovich
ATLANTA CONSTITUTION

MIKE LUCKOVICH
Courtesy Atlanta Constitution

ANNETTE BALESTERI
Courtesy Antioch Daily Ledger (Calif.)

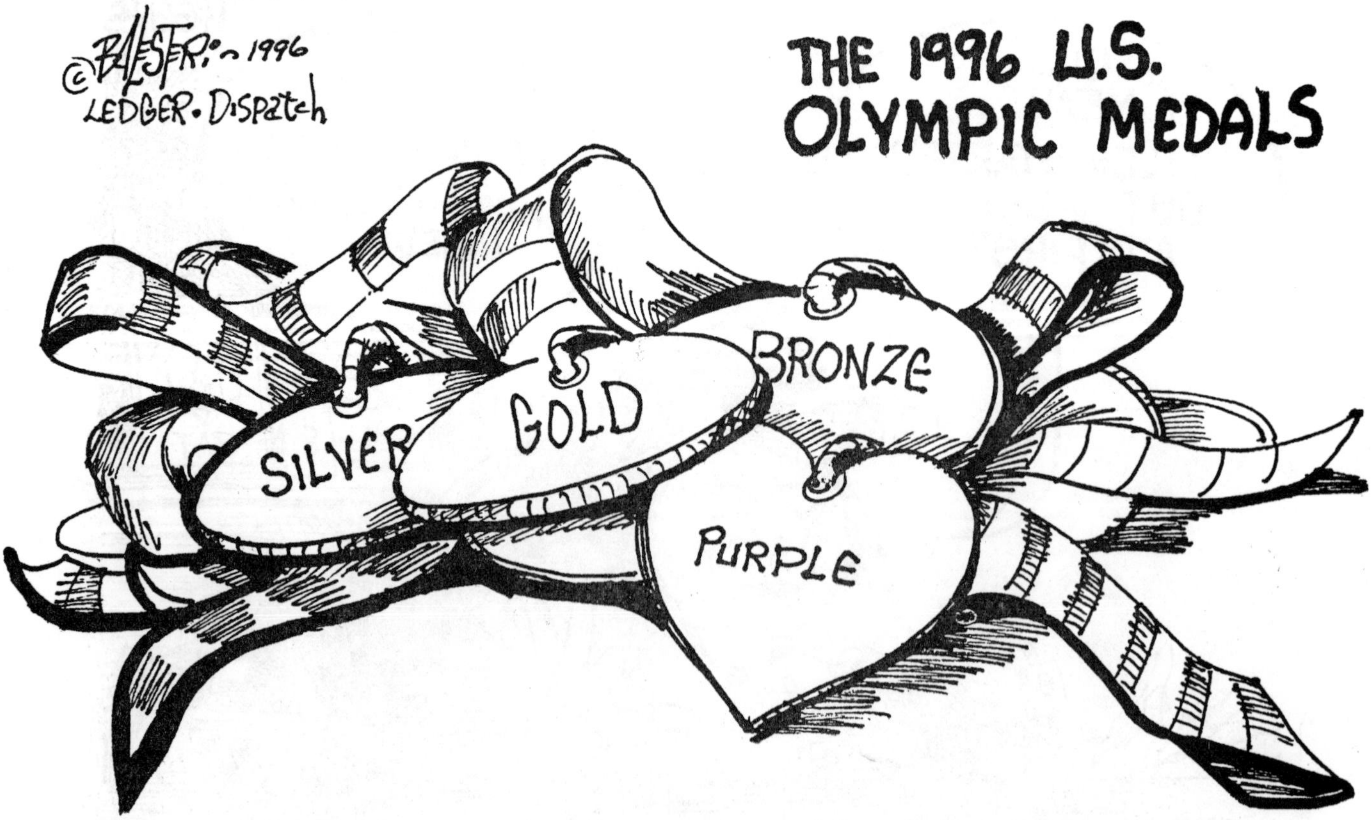
©BALESTERI 1996
LEDGER·Dispatch
THE 1996 U.S. OLYMPIC MEDALS
SILVER
GOLD
BRONZE
PURPLE

WAYNE STAYSKAL
Courtesy Tampa Tribune

ANDY DONATO
Courtesy Toronto Sun

J. R. ROSE
Courtesy Byrd Newspapers

S. C. RAWLS
Courtesy Rockdale Citizen

CHESTER COMMODORE, SR.
Courtesy Chicago Daily Defender

ED COLLEY
Courtesy Old Colony Memorial (Mass.)

STEVE HILL
Courtesy Kansas City Star

JOHN KOVALIC
Courtesy Wisconsin State Journal

AN NFL OWNER WRITES AN OPEN LETTER TO THE FANS...

JOHN SPENCER
Courtesy Philadelphia Business Journal

JIM BORGMAN
Courtesy Cincinnati Enquirer

STRIKE ZONE

SPIT ZONE

AMERICAN JUSTICE: A COMPARISON

JIM BUSH
Courtesy Providence Journal Bulletin

KISSED CLASSMATE.
RECEIVED: SUSPENSION

SMOOCH

PTOOOEY

SPAT IN UMPIRE'S FACE.
RECEIVED: A STANDING OVATION

JAMES CASCIARI
Courtesy Vero Beach Press Journal

CHAN LOWE
Courtesy The News/Sun-Sentinel (Fla.)

. . . and Other Issues

A discrimination suit was filed against Texaco by black employees who accused the company of consistently discriminating in hiring and promotion practices. The suit ended with a $176 million settlement. A similar suit, which was settled to minority satisfaction, was filed against Denny's, a restaurant chain.

Researchers at N.A.S.A. reported that a rock from Mars showed evidence that bacteria might have lived in it billions of years ago. Pope John Paul II declared that evolution is "more than just a theory" and is compatible with the Christian faith.

Federal agents surrounded members of the anti-government Freemen in Montana and after a long standoff forced the group to surrender without bloodshed. A much-publicized auction of personal items that once belonged to Jacqueline Kennedy Onassis brought millions of dollars.

Jessica Dobroff, a seven-year-old pilot, was killed in a crash while trying to become the youngest person to fly across the U.S.

Notables who died in 1996 included Francois Mitterrand, Greer Garson, Minnie Pearl, George Burns, Ella Fitzgerald, Gene Kelly, Carl Sagan, Spiro Agnew, Pete Rozelle, John Chancellor . . . and editorial cartoonist Randy Wicks.

ROBERT ARIAIL
Courtesy The State (S.C.)

CAMELOOT

IF TREES COULD TALK

THE BOTTOM LINE...

STEVE KELLEY
Courtesy San Diego Union

EUGENE PAYNE
Courtesy Charlotte Observer

JIM BORGMAN
Courtesy Cincinnati Enquirer

CARLOS GARY
Courtesy Star-Gazette (N.Y.)

JEFF PARKER
Courtesy Florida Today

JOHN DEERING
Courtesy Arkansas Democrat-Gazette

JIM MCCLOSKEY
Courtesy Staunton Daily News Leader

BARBARA BRANDON
Courtesy Universal Press Syndicate

STEVE ARMSTRONG
Courtesy Progress-Index (Va.)

BRUMSIC BRANDON
Courtesy Florida Today

RANDY WICKS
Courtesy Valencia Signal (Calif.)

MIKE THOMPSON
Courtesy State Journal-Register (Ill.)

JERRY BARNETT
Courtesy Indianapolis News

SCOTT BATEMAN
Courtesy Daily Tidings (Ore.

GARY BROOKINS
Courtesy Richmond Times-Dispatch

VIC CANTONE
Courtesy King Features/North America Syndicate

UNDER THE INFLUENCE

MIKE THOMPSON
Courtesy State Journal-Register (Ill.)

DAVID GRANLUND
Courtesy Middlesex News

STEVE BREEN
Courtesy Asbury Park Press (N.J.)

194

CHUCK ASAY
Courtesy Colorado Springs Gazette Telegraph

TOM GIBB
Courtesy Rothco

JOSEPH F. MAHONEY
Courtesy The Enterprise (Mass.)

ROGER SCHILLERSTROM
Courtesy Crain Communications

ANN TELNAES
Courtesy North America Syndicate

JIM BORGMAN
Courtesy Cincinnati Enquirer

JOHN SHERFFIUS
Courtesy Ventura Star-Free Press

JERRY HOLBERT
Courtesy Boston Herald

S. C. RAWLS
Courtesy Rockdale Citizen

S. C. RAWLS
Courtesy Rockdale Citizen

JOE HELLER
Courtesy Green Bay Press-Gazette

ON BEING TOO YOUNG TO FLY

"MY REFRIGERATOR JUST WON'T SEEM THE SAME..."

J. R. ROSE
Courtesy Byrd Newspapers

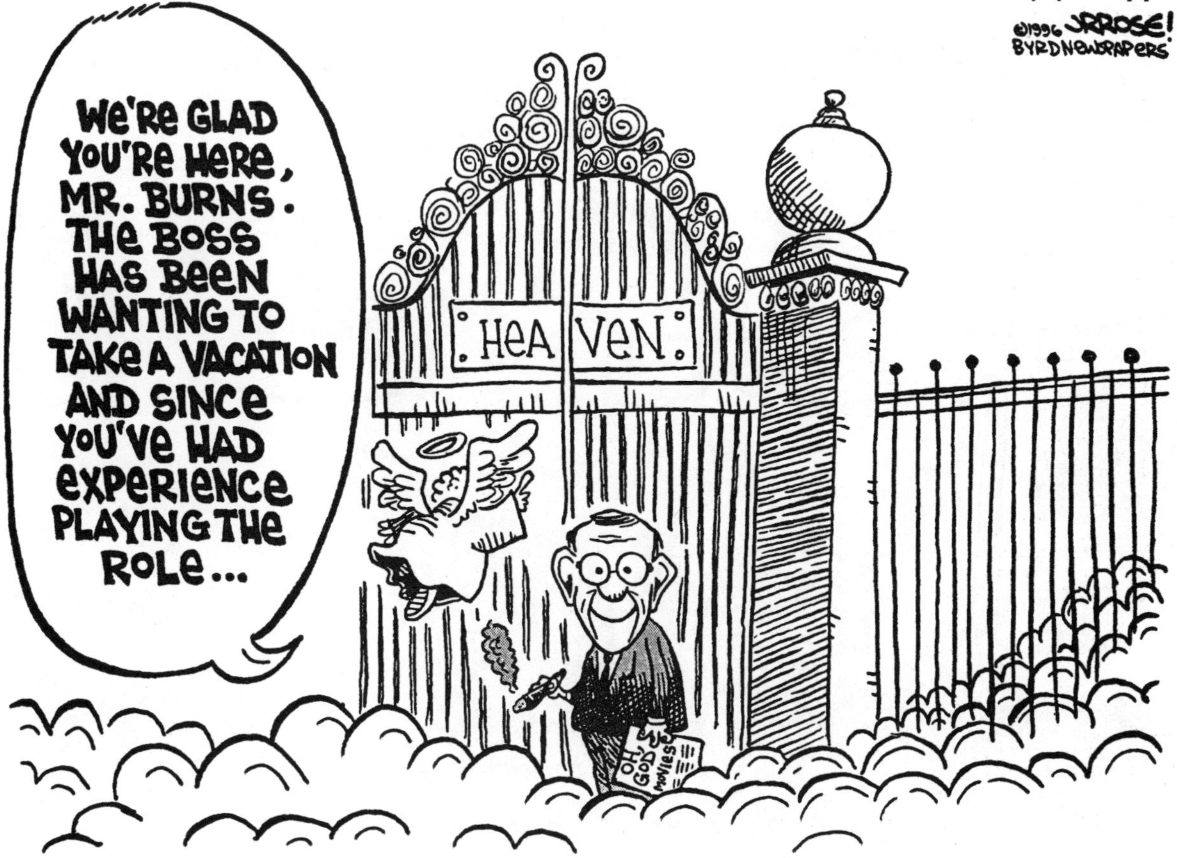
©1996 JRROSE! BYRDNEWSPAPERS
WE'RE GLAD YOU'RE HERE, MR. BURNS. THE BOSS HAS BEEN WANTING TO TAKE A VACATION AND SINCE YOU'VE HAD EXPERIENCE PLAYING THE ROLE...
HEAVEN

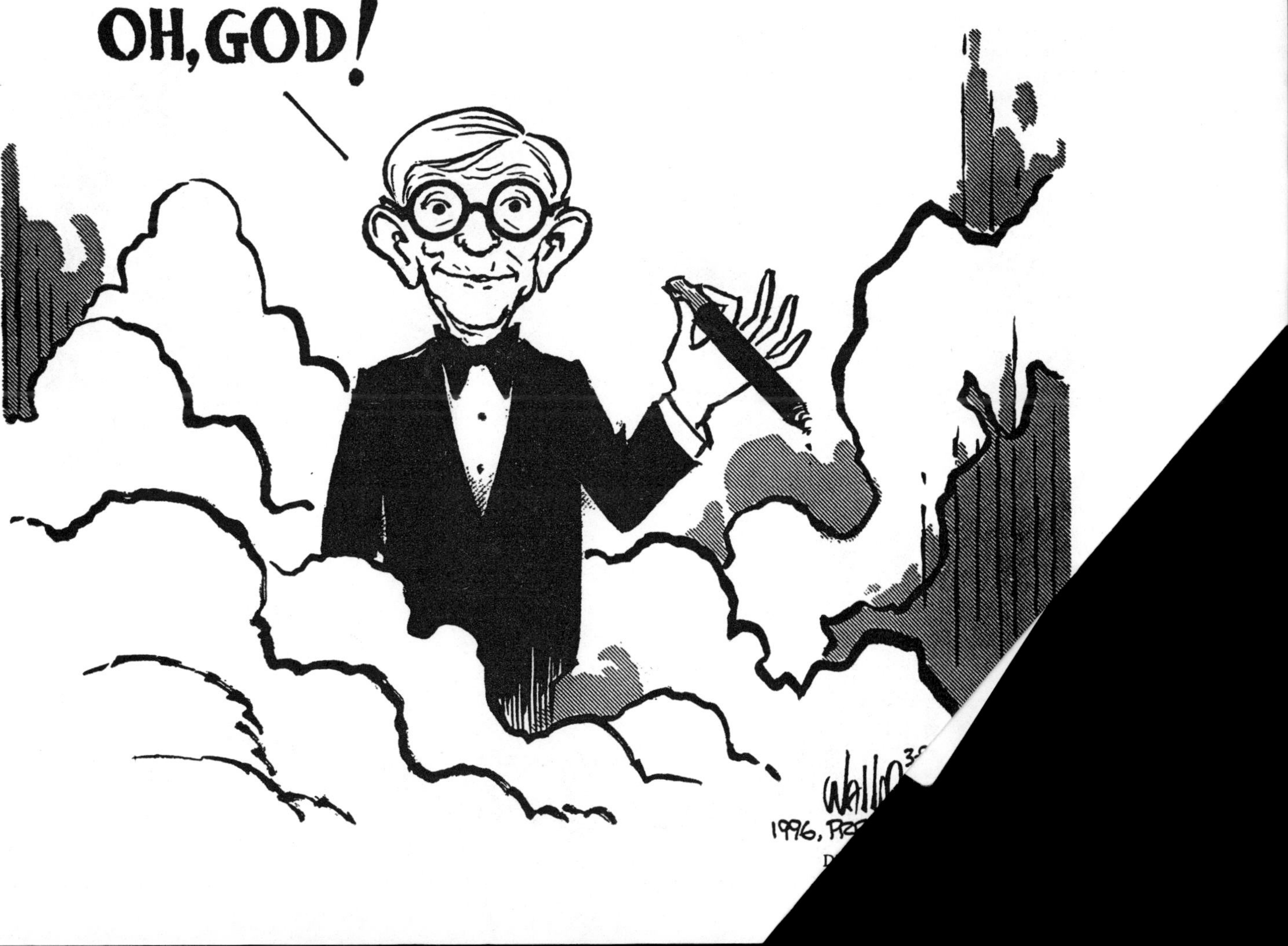
OH, GOD!

WALT HANDELSMAN
Courtesy Times-Picayune (N.O.)

JOHN SHERFFIUS
Courtesy Ventura Star-Free Press

WICKS © THE NEWHALL SIGNAL 1996

…ICK WALLMEYER
Courtesy Long Beach Pre…

Past Award Winners

NATIONAL HEADLINERS CLUB AWARD

1938—C. D. Batchelor, New York Daily News
1939—John Knott, Dallas News
1940—Herbert Block, NEA
1941—Charles H. Sykes, Philadelphia Evening Ledger
1942—Jerry Doyle, Philadelphia Record
1943—Vaughn Shoemaker, Chicago Daily News
1944—Roy Justus, Sioux City Journal
1945—F. O. Alexander, Philadelphia Bulletin
1946—Hank Barrow, Associated Press
1947—Cy Hungerford, Pittsburgh Post Gazette
1948—Tom Little, Nashville Tennessean
1949—Bruce Russell, Los Angeles Times
1950—Dorman Smith, NEA
1951—C. G. Werner, Indianapolis Star
1952—John Fischetti, NEA
1953—James T. Berryman and
　　　Gib Crocket, Washington Star
1954—Scott Long, Minneapolis Tribune
1955—Leo Thiele, Los Angeles Mirror News
1956—John Milt Morris, Associated Press
1957—Frank Miller, Des Moines Register
1958—Burris Jenkins, Jr., New York Journal American
1959—Karl Hubenthal, Los Angeles Examiner
1960—Don Hesse, St. Louis Globe Democrat
1961—L. D. Warren, Cincinnati Enquirer
1962—Franklin Morse, Los Angeles Mirror
1963—Charles Bissell, Nashville Tennessean
1964—Lou Grant, Oakland Tribune
1965—Merle R. Tingley, London (Ont.) Free Press
1966—Hugh Haynie, Louisville Courier Journal
1967—Jim Berry, NEA
1968—Warren King, New York News
1969—Larry Barton, Toledo Blade
1970—Bill Crawford, NEA
1971—Ray Osrin, Cleveland Plain Dealer
1972—Jacob Burck, Chicago Sun Times
1973—Ranan Lurie, New York Times
1974—Tom Darcy, Newsday
1975—Bill Sanders, Milwaukee Journal
1976—No award given
1977—Paul Szep, Boston Globe
1978—Dwane Powell, Raleigh News and Observer
1979—Pat Oliphant, Washington Star
1980—Don Wright, Miami News
1981—Bill Garner, Memphis Commercial Appeal
1982—Mike Peters, Dayton Daily News
1983—Doug Marlette, Charlotte Observer
1984—Steve Benson, Arizona Republic
1985—Bill Day, Detroit Free Press
1986—Mike Keefe, Denver Post
1987—Mike Peters, Dayton Daily News
1988—Doug Marlette, Charlotte Observer
1989—Walt Handelsman, Scranton Times
1990—Robert Ariail, The State
1991—Jim Borgman, Cincinnati Enquirer
1992—Mike Luckovich, Atlanta Constitution
1993—Walt Handelsman, New Orleans Times Picayune
1994—Mike Peters, Dayton Daily News
1995—Rob Rogers, Pittsburgh Post-Gazette
1996—Jimmy Margulies, The Record, New Jersey

PULITZER PRIZE

1922—Rollin Kirby, New York World
1923—No award given
1924—J. N. Darling, New York Herald Tribune
1925—Rollin Kirby, New York World
1926—D. R. Fitzpatrick, St. Louis Post-Dispatch
1927—Nelson Harding, Brooklyn Eagle
1928—Nelson Harding, Brooklyn Eagle
1929—Rollin Kirby, New York World
1930—Charles Macauley, Brooklyn Eagle
1931—Edmund Duffy, Baltimore Sun
1932—John T. McCutcheon, Chicago Tribune
1933—H. M. Talburt, Washington Daily News
1934—Edmund Duffy, Baltimore Sun
1935—Ross A. Lewis, Milwaukee Journal
1936—No award given
1937—C. D. Batchelor, New York Daily News
1938—Vaughn Shoemaker, Chicago Daily News
1939—Charles G. Werner, Daily Oklahoman
1940—Edmund Duffy, Baltimore Sun
1941—Jacob Burck, Chicago Times
1942—Herbert L. Block, NEA
1943—Jay N. Darling, New York Herald Tribune
1944—Clifford K. Berryman, Washington Star
1945—Bill Mauldin, United Features Syndicate
1946—Bruce Russell, Los Angeles Times
1947—Vaughn Shoemaker, Chicago Daily News
1948—Reuben L. ("Rube") Goldberg, New York Sun
1949—Lute Pease, Newark Evening News
1950—James T. Berryman, Washington Star
1951—Reginald W. Manning, Arizona Republic
1952—Fred L. Packer, New York Mirror
1953—Edward D. Kuekes, Cleveland Plain Dealer
1954—Herbert L. Block, Washington Post
1955—Daniel R. Fitzpatrick, St. Louis Post-Dispatch
1956—Robert York, Louisville Times
1957—Tom Little, Nashville Tennessean
1958—Bruce M. Shanks, Buffalo Evening News
1959—Bill Mauldin, St. Louis Post-Dispatch
1960—No award given
1961—Carey Orr, Chicago Tribune
1962—Edmund S. Valtman, Hartford Times

1963—Frank Miller, Des Moines Register
1964—Paul Conrad, Denver Post
1965—No award given
1966—Don Wright, Miami News
1967—Patrick B. Oliphant, Denver Post
1968—Eugene Gray Payne, Charlotte Observer
1969—John Fischetti, Chicago Daily News
1970—Thomas F. Darcy, Newsday
1971—Paul Conrad, Los Angeles Times
1972—Jeffrey K. MacNelly, Richmond News Leader
1973—No award given
1974—Paul Szep, Boston Globe
1975—Garry Trudeau, Universal Press Syndicate
1976—Tony Auth, Philadelphia Enquirer
1977—Paul Szep, Boston Globe
1978—Jeff MacNelly, Richmond News Leader
1979—Herbert Block, Washington Post
1980—Don Wright, Miami News
1981—Mike Peters, Dayton Daily News
1982—Ben Sargent, Austin American-Statesman
1983—Dick Locher, Chicago Tribune
1984—Paul Conrad, Los Angeles Times
1985—Jeff MacNelly, Chicago Tribune
1986—Jules Feiffer, Universal Press Syndicate
1987—Berke Breathed, Washington Post Writers Group
1988—Doug Marlette, Atlanta Constitution
1989—Jack Higgins, Chicago Sun-Times
1990—Tom Toles, Buffalo News
1991—Jim Borgman, Cincinnati Enquirer
1992—Signe Wilkinson, Philadelphia Daily News
1993—Steve Benson, Arizona Republic
1994—Michael Ramirez, Memphis Commercial Appeal
1995—Mike Luckovich, Atlanta Constitution
1996—Jim Morin, Miami Herald

NATIONAL NEWSPAPER AWARD / CANADA

1949—Jack Boothe, Toronto Globe and Mail
1950—James G. Reidford, Montreal Star
1951—Len Norris, Vancouver Sun
1952—Robert La Palme, Le Devoir, Montreal
1953—Robert W. Chambers, Halifax Chronicle-Herald
1954—John Collins, Montreal Gazette
1955—Merle R. Tingley, London Free Press
1956—James G. Reidford, Toronto Globe and Mail
1957—James G. Reidford, Toronto Globe and Mail
1958—Raoul Hunter, Le Soleil, Quebec
1959—Duncan Macpherson, Toronto Star
1960—Duncan Macpherson, Toronto Star
1961—Ed McNally, Montreal Star
1962—Duncan Macpherson, Toronto Star

1963—Jan Kamienski, Winnipeg Tribune
1964—Ed McNally, Montreal Star
1965—Duncan Macpherson, Toronto Star
1966—Robert W. Chambers, Halifax Chronicle-Herald
1967—Raoul Hunter, Le Soleil, Quebec
1968—Roy Peterson, Vancouver Sun
1969—Edward Uluschak, Edmonton Journal
1970—Duncan Macpherson, Toronto Daily Star
1971—Yardley Jones, Toronto Star
1972—Duncan Macpherson, Toronto Star
1973—John Collins, Montreal Gazette
1974—Blaine, Hamilton Spectator
1975—Roy Peterson, Vancouver Sun
1976—Andy Donato, Toronto Sun
1977—Terry Mosher, Montreal Gazette
1978—Terry Mosher, Montreal Gazette
1979—Edd Uluschak, Edmonton Journal
1980—Vic Roschkov, Toronto Star
1981—Tom Innes, Calgary Herald
1982—Blaine, Hamilton Spectator
1983—Dale Cummings, Winnipeg Free Press
1984—Roy Peterson, Vancouver Sun
1985—Ed Franklin, Toronto Globe and Mail
1986—Brian Gable, Regina Leader Post
1987—Raffi Anderian, Ottawa Citizen
1988—Vance Rodewalt, Calgary Herald
1989—Cameron Cardow, Regina Leader-Post
1990—Roy Peterson, Vancouver Sun
1991—Guy Badeaux, Le Droit, Ottawa
1992—Bruce Mackinnon, Halifax Herald
1993—Bruce Mackinnon, Halifax Herald
1994—Roy Peterson, Vancouver Sun
1995—Brian Gable, Toronto Globe and Mail

FISCHETTI AWARD

1982—Lee Judge, Kansas City Times
1983—Bill DeOre, Dallas Morning News
1984—Tom Toles, Buffalo News
1985—Scott Willis, Dallas Times-Herald
1986—Doug Marlette, Charlotte Observer
1987—Dick Locher, Chicago Tribune
1988—Arthur Bok, Akron Beacon-Journal
1989—Lambert Der, Greenville News
1990—Jeff Stahler, Cincinnati Post
1991—Mike Keefe, Denver Post
1992—Doug Marlette, New York Newsday
1993—Bill Schorr, Kansas City Star
1994—John Deering, Arkansas Democrat-Gazette
1995—Stuart Carlson, Milwaukee Journal Sentinel
1996—Jimmy Margulies, The Record, New Jersey

Index of Cartoonists

Aguila, Dani, 86, 161
Anderson, Kirk, 78, 138
Anderson, Nick, 92, 102, 170
Ariail, Robert, 82, 158, 185
Armstrong, Steve, 190
Asay, Chuck, 124, 141, 195

Babin, Rex, 37, 73, 100
Badeaux, Guy, 98 (2)
Balesteri, Annette, 135, 178
Barnett, Jerry, 113, 126, 192
Bateman, Scott, 110, 192
Beattie, Bruce, 98, 126
Beck, Tom, 49
Bennett, Clay, 57, 113, 136
Benson, Tim, 107
Berry, Jim, 34, 46, 49, 90, 94
Bish, Randy, 50, 152
Bloom, Neal, 91
Boileau, Linda, 53, 69
Boldt, Thomas A., 45, 93, 96
Borgman, Jim, 43, 151, 183, 188, 197
Branch, John, 134, 149
Brandon, Barbara, 190
Brandon, Brumsic, Jr., 62, 190
Breen, Steve, 116, 186, 194
Brewer, Mark, 20, 99
Brookins, Gary, 26, 83, 120, 143, 192
Buckley, Jerry, 64, 87
Bush, Jim, 183

Cammuso, Frank, 63, 65
Campbell, Sandy, 84, back cover
Cantone, Vic, 76, 193
Casciari, James, 145, 184
Cavna, Michael, 176, 178
Cleaves, Ann, 104
Colley, Ed, 148, 181
Commodore, Chester, 180
Conrad, Paul, 45, 75, 136
Curatolo, Fred, 97, 164
Curtis, Chris, 125

Danby, George, 50, 59, 108
Daniel, Charles, 23, 122, 140
Deering, John, 47, 189
DeRosier, John, 69, 159
Donar, David, 43
Donato, Andy, 14, 164, 179
Dornfried, Bob, 119, 121
Draughon, Dennis, 40, 134, 139

Duffy, Brian, 16, 72, 128
Dunagin, Ralph, 38, 157 (2)

Engelhardt, Tom, 72, 171
Englehart, Bob, 30 (2), 115
Fell, Paul, 147
Fischer, Ed, 109
Flint, Bubba, 42, 109
Fox, Gill, 141
Fresquet, Lazaro, 86, 154
Fuller, Jake, 33, 95

Gable, Brian, 9, 62, 89, 99
Gamble, Ed, 86, 108, 128, 160, 169
Garner, Bill, 48, 83
Gary, Carlos, 188
Germano, Eddie, 115 (2)
Gibb, Tom, 195
Gillett, Michael, 117
Gorrell, Bob, 32, 54, 156
Grahame, Neil, 107
Granlund, Dave, 88, 161, 173, 175, 194
Grant, Lou, 116, 186
Grasdal, James, 100, 103
Greenberg, Steve, 104, 132

Handelsman, Walt, 20, 52, 146, 202
Hartman, Tim, 58
Harvell, Roger, 67, 88
Harville, Vic, 27, 155
Heller, Joe, 54, 199, 200
Henrikson, Art, 76
Higgins, Jack, 32, 58, 173, 177
Hill, Draper, 2, 53, 70
Hill, Steve, 181
Hitch, David, 91
Hoffecker, Joe, 106, 111
Hogan, Bill, 165, 168
Holbert, Jerry, 26, 138, 198
Hulme, Etta, 30, 101, 127, 159

Jones, Clay, 20, 79
Jordan, Jim, 89
Jurden, Jack, 70, 148

Kallaugher, Kevin, 118, 127, front cover
Keefe, Mike, 94, 106, 144
Kelley, Steve, 52, 135, 187
King, Alan, 95, 154, 160
Knudsen, John, 34, 94
Kollinger, Rick, 25, 177

INDEX OF CARTOONISTS

Koterba, Jeff, 84, 137, 160
Kovalic, John, 182

Lait, Steven, 21, 60
Landgren, Don, Jr., 171
Lang, Bob, 157
Lange, Jim, 34, 68
Larrick, James, 71, 174
Lee, Don, 75
Lindstrom, Steve, 78, 134
Little, Jeff, 117
Locher, Dick, 15, 18, 22, 55, 153
Long, Joe, 74, 118
Lowe, Chan, 24, 77, 184
Luckovich, Mike, 28, 106, 133, 152, 178

MacGregor, Doug, 32, 42, 156, 172
MacNelly, Jeff, 55, 114, 122, 145, 150
Mahoney, Joseph F., 196
Majeski, Joe, 42, 92
Margulies, Jimmy, 10, 11, 31, 102, 108
Markstein, Gary, 80, 132
Marquis, Don, 200
Marshall, John, 66, 111
Mayes, Malcolm, 67, 96, 163, 168
McBride, Steve, 19, 77, 79
McCloskey, James, 48, 189
McClure, Hank, 82, 90
McCoy, Gary, 16, 27
McCoy, Glenn, 17, 61, 152
McLeod, Jack, 68, 140
Mercado, James, 74, 144
Morin, Jim, 7, 60, 80, 81, 103
Murphy, Dan, 90, 164

Nease, Stephen, 164, 167
Nickel, Scott, 56

OBrion, Chris, 39, 50, 147
Ohman, Jack, 12, 51, 63, 66, 71

Parker, Jeff, 58, 188
Payne, Eugene, 119, 161, 187
Peters, Mike, 33, 35, 44, 87, 153
Peterson, Roy, 162 (2), 165, 167
Priggee, Milt, 49, 53, 154
Pritchard, Denny, 64, 110, 166

Quast, Bruce, 150

Rall, Ted, 105, 112
Ramirez, Michael, 8, 44, 56, 114, 130

Rand, Wes, 118, 149
Rank, Joe, 62
Rawls, S. C., 180, 198, 199
Regalia, Douglas, 141
Rice, Patrick, 124, 148
Rich, Bob, 126
Richards, Jon, 158
Ritter, Mike, 36, 39, 47
Rogers, Rob, 35, 59, 146
Rose, J. R., 23, 180, 201

Sagastegui, Oswaldo, 85, 159
Sattler, Dave, 105, 128
Schillerstrom, Roger, 196
Sebastian, Fred, 176
Sheneman, Drew, 176
Sherffius, John, 186, 197, 202
Smith, Eric, 46, 64
Smith, Mike, 170, 172
Soller, Edgar, 63
Spencer, John, 112, 182
Stahler, Jeff, 140, 144, 170
Stantis, Scott, 24, 40, 130, 139
Stayskal, Wayne, 37, 179
Stein, Ed, 36, 65, 74
Stephanos, Dale, 29, 31
Streeter, Mark, 21, 61
Stroot, Wayne, 78, 121
Summers, Dana, 93, 120, 150
Szep, Paul, 52, 90, 142, 156

Telnaes, Ann, 26, 46, 196
Templeton, Stephen, 38, 69
Thompson, Mike, 28, 191, 193
Thornhill, Mark, 68, 142
Tingley, Merle, 166 (2)
Trever, John, 18, 29, 155

Van Assche, Sven, 23
Varvel, Gary, 123, 125, 129
Vitello, Alan, 129

Wallmeyer, Dick, 201
Walters, Kirk, 19, 25
Wells, Clyde, 17, 131, 174
Whitehead, Bill, 46
Wicks, Randy, 135, 191
Willis, Scott, 41, 136
Wright, Dick, 22, 38
Wright, Larry, 118, 149
Wuerker, M., 133

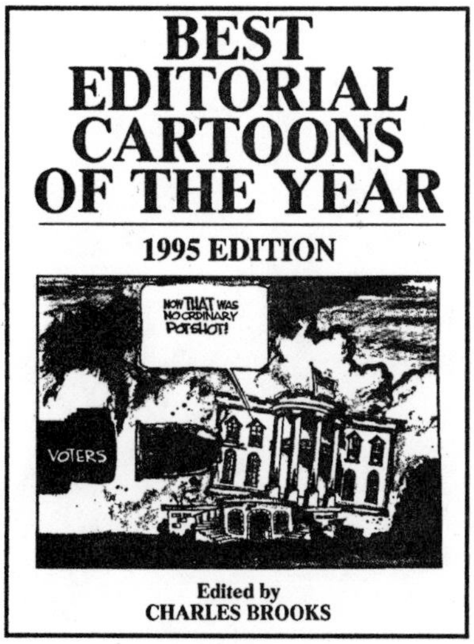
BEST EDITORIAL CARTOONS OF THE YEAR
1995 EDITION
NOW THAT WAS NO ORDINARY POTSHOT!
VOTERS
Edited by
CHARLES BROOKS

COMPLETE YOUR CARTOON COLLECTION

Previous editions of this timeless series are available for those wishing to update their collection of the most provocative moments of the past twenty years. In the early days the topics were the oil crisis, Richard Nixon's presidency, Watergate, and the Vietnam War. Over time the cartoonists and their subjects have changed right along with presidential administrations. These days those subjects have been replaced by the Clinton administration, Bosnia, O. J. Simpson, and the environment. But in the end, the wit and wisdom of the editorial cartoonists has prevailed. And on the pages of these op-ed galleries one can find memories and much more from the nation's best cartoonists.

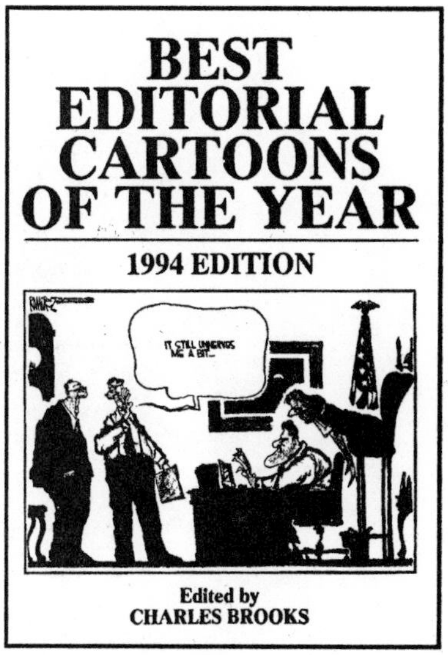
BEST EDITORIAL CARTOONS OF THE YEAR
1994 EDITION
Edited by
CHARLES BROOKS

Select from the following supply of past editions

______ 1972 Edition	$18.95 hc	______ 1982 Edition	$14.95 pb	______ 1991 Edition	$14.95 pb
______ 1974 Edition	$18.95 hc	1983 Edition	out of print	______ 1992 Edition	$14.95 pb
______ 1975 Edition	$18.95 hc	______ 1984 Edition	$14.95 pb	______ 1993 Edition	$14.95 pb
______ 1976 Edition	$18.95 hc	______ 1985 Edition	$14.95 pb	______ 1994 Edition	$14.95 pb
______ 1977 Edition	$18.95 hc	______ 1986 Edition	$14.95 pb	______ 1995 Edition	$14.95 pb
1978 Edition	out of print	______ 1987 Edition	$14.95 pb	______ 1996 Edition	$14.95 pb
1979 Edition	out of print	______ 1988 Edition	$14.95 pb	______ Please add me to the list of standing orders for future editions.	
______ 1980 Edition	$18.95 hc	1989 Edition	out of print		
______ 1981 Edition	$14.95 pb	______ 1990 Edition	$14.95 pb		

Please include $2.50 for 4th Class Postage and handling or $4.75 for UPS Ground Shipment plus $.75 for each additional copy ordered.*

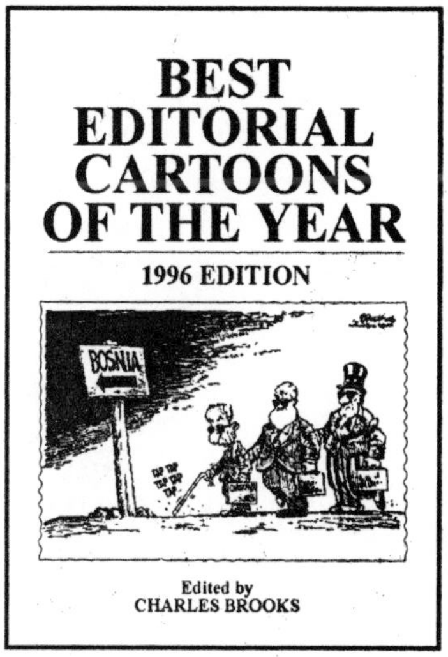
BEST EDITORIAL CARTOONS OF THE YEAR
1996 EDITION
BOSNIA
Edited by
CHARLES BROOKS

Total enclosed: ____________________

NAME ____

ADDRESS ____

CITY ____________________ STATE ________ ZIP __________

Make checks payable to:

PELICAN PUBLISHING COMPANY
P.O. Box 3110, Dept. 6BEC
Gretna, Louisiana 70054

CREDIT CARD ORDERS CALL 1-800-843-1724 or 1-888-5-PELICAN

* Jefferson Parish residents add 8¾% tax. All other Louisiana residents add 4% tax.